THE GATEWAY

of LIBERATION

MARY GRAY

NEW AGE PRESS
4636 Vineta
La Canada, Calif. 91011

Second Edition

Printed in the United States of America by—
DeVorss & Co., 1641 Lincoln Blvd., Santa Monica, Calif. 90404

To THE SONS OF FIRE
IN ALL WORLDS

Note:

Parts I & II—The Training
of the Probationary Path—were
printed in *The Herald of the Star*
in 1924. Part III was written in
1927, and Part IV in 1931.

Mary Gray,
Casa de Paz,
Ojai, California.

CONTENTS

FOREWORD

There come into incarnation in various countries, certain souls who have reached a point in evolution where they turn their faces steadfastly from the world towards that Mountain of Light which some call God.

In the resources of worldly pleasure, of human happiness, of knowledge or of power, they find no comfort. They are goaded by the sense of being trapped in a world which offers them no satisfying purpose for living, no food for the soul.

They see that happiness here endures not, power fails, pleasure palls, and they are filled, therefore, with unceasing restlessness of mind and spirit. With constant reiteration, the great question *why, and to what end,* arises in their souls.

It is for such that what follows is written. For those who know that personal happiness passes and that power but rouses hatred; it is for those who desire earnestly to know the purpose of life; the reason for man's existence upon this planet; something of the plan and the way of fulfillment; that these pages are offered. Those who are still content with their daily round of duties, pleasures, services, as yet need no further aid.

But upon the many crossroads of our planet—its by-ways and high-ways—travel those who seek the Gateway of Liberation, at the end of the Path of Initiation. In some long past time the seed of occult truth was planted in their hearts, a vision of the gateway which leads to the shining land of Brotherhood cast a light upon their souls which urged them life after life to seek the reality which lay behind the vision.

Perchance some wise teacher gave them knowledge of the Pearl of pearls, and led their still human feet to the entrance of that way which leads to divinity. And now today there rises again within the imperative need to storm the rocky heights which guard the citadel, which, when attained, makes man no longer son of man, but Son of God.

That the way may be a little clearer, that the search may be a little more eager, that the realities may shine more clear, these pages are inscribed.

For above and beyond all things, if the Path is to be found, and if the Path is to be trod, the vision of the goal like a lodestar must rouse in the soul that holy fire which alone can give the power to achieve.

PART I
The Path of Probation

CHAPTER I
The Awakening

In order that man might sooner break through the thrall of passing pleasures, and hearken to the laws of evolution, the great Teachers have again and again spoken the Truth, that life of itself is pain and that no lasting happiness may here be found.

If one really grasps this fact and ceases to follow the will-o'-the-wisp—ever elusive—of personal happiness, the mind lies open to receive the Truth: the purpose of life as seen from the consciousness of the Infinite. This Truth is visioned by the seers from age to age for man's guidance when he feels the need arise for light upon his path.

When the hour comes in which a human soul truly recognizes its bondage and longs for freedom, then does the mind open to receive the light, shut away heretofore by the constant search for earthly happiness.

Some do not reach this point until the period of possible earthly happiness passes, and old age approaches. Then, as they look back upon their lives and upon the past, they wonder what has been gained by this succession of generations, each spending its life caring for and preparing for the next, century after century.

Nations rise and fall. The progress of civilization is uncertain and unstable. A cataclysm comes, wars, disasters, earthquakes, and the fruits of many years, of many lives, of many nations, are swept away. What is the value of this human struggle? What then is the purpose—what the law?

When man awakens to a need for a knowledge of the law, when the mind is thus open, then may be given the true understanding of evolution, and the final purpose of human incarnation.

It is a high purpose—the gaining of mind—the achievement of independent judgment through the knowledge of good and evil.

This gained gives to man the power of creative thought, the power of Kriyashakti (the power of divine Creation), of the forming of universes various in kind, method, and evolution.

This is the power that the devas or angels have not—and until they gain it they are the servants of those who have it.

The Holy Spirit—Mahat—alone has the power to create, and it is the creative function upon the physical plane which is the gift of the Holy Spirit and promise of the future creative power on every plane as man learns the secret of the control and the use of sex, speech, and thought.

This unfoldment of creative power under the Third Logos comes only as a sequence to the unfoldment of the powers of Will and Wisdom under the First and Second Logoi which has been done in past systems. It is the critical period of evolution when man ventures his eternal life to win "salvation", the mastery of his own spirit, the awakening of the Godhood within him.

To gain his heritage of conscious divinity and the divine attributes of creative power which follow upon this, he must be immersed in matter, cut away from the inner wisdom, from spiritual light, and from his consciousness of God, that he may unfold vision, light, and the Godhead within himself. He must meet evil, which is but the other pole of good, negative and positive, attraction and repulsion, in order that he may know it, may control it and so may use it.

For evil, so-called, is involution, a necessary part of all cosmic development in the earlier stages, associated with the descent into matter, the assimilation of form. That which we know as evil is evil only on the evolutionary arc when man is rising out of matter to his Source, to unveil the God within. The evolutionary forces represent evil on the involutionary arc, just as the involutionary forces represent evil on the evolutionary arc. Evil is that which is a hindrance to achieving the purposes of the soul at any given point of development.

We must vision man's career as an arc of descent and ascent. During the descent into matter he is veiling himself in denser and denser form in which the God is hidden; he is building a form, more and more selfish and self-centred, more and more powerful, more and more separate, in which he may enclose the Divine Flame that it may gain isolation. Only thus separated and thus detached at once from its Source, the Universal Godhead, and from its fellows, can it gain conscious, separate, individual Divinity.

Therefore, on the descending or involutionary arc, the law of man must be selfishness, isolation, combat, until the form is vigorous and dense enough an animal to safeguard his isolation and to hide effectually his divinity. This is the period of the savage or of the animal which is governed by the law of the survival of the fittest, that the bodies may become powerful.

This accomplished, man is given his heritage of mind; the spark of divine ideation, logic, reason. As he slowly evolves mind, he evolves the power which shall give him control ultimately of the creative forces of the universe and of himself, as mirroring the Macrocosm in the Microcosm, as reflecting God in man.

The law of the evolutionary arc, when man seeks to use the animal he has built to manifest his divine powers, when he seeks to become the mirror of God, must be the law of sacrifice and unselfishness.

During the unfoldment of mind, surrounded by all forces, both good and evil, man's path is difficult. He knows not good from evil and manifests both.

The test of his insight will come in his choice. It will be proved if he can choose the evolutionary forces which will carry him upward to his divinity. If he chooses the involutionary forces he endangers his heritage and at the time of ultimate choice he may choose destruction, not salvation and Godhead.

Manas, the higher mind, of itself gives knowledge, insight, independent creative power. The gaining of the powers of mind is the purpose of our present evolution.

It is a long and arduous task, lasting through many aeons, as man, driven by desire, checked by pain, goaded by necessity, slowly awakens from his mental lethargy, from his heedless response to impulse.

At last, to escape from painful conditions about him, or to attain his desires, he begins to use his intelligence. Man in his early development is by nature lazy, both physically and mentally, and shrinks from protracted thought, or from the continued action required by a plan, mind born, which must be carried out.

He must, therefore, in earlier days constantly be driven by
three goads, fear, pain and hatred. These are aroused in him
by the conflict in the world; by the cruelty of his conditions;
by hunger, sickness, loss, want, cold and all other human ills.

Only such goads will drive inert minds into the processes
of sustained thought. And as sustained thought alone can
unfold the powers of mind, these goads we find throughout
much of the earlier stages of human life. All institutions
which tend to relieve man from the necessity of thought, or
to repress in him independent thought, are against evolution.

In the beginning of the development of mind, it is not
important how a man thinks, or what causes him to think.
The one essential is to develop the faculty of thought; and
as the savage man is too undeveloped to respond to the higher
motives of ambition, desire for achievement, spiritual aspiration or unselfish love, he must be reached by the only spurs
that he can recognize.

As the greatest virtues the race knows, power, compassion
and knowledge, lotus-like spring from the roots of wrath,
lust and greed, so the unfoldment of the divine quality of
mind is spurred in its beginning by fear and hatred and pain.

As man evolves, the goads of fear and hate are replaced by
others more suited to the evolving spirit. But throughout
evolution on the physical plane, pain remains as the great
friend and teacher of man, refining the bodies, uplifting the
soul, guarding him from error and from false paths, and
leading him by slow steps to the heights of self-sacrifice,
which shall at last make him divine.

Yet, withal, since the greatest danger ultimately to the
race lies in the unfoldment of mind not dominated by the
softening influences of compassion and spiritual wisdom—
buddhi—throughout the ages come the spiritual teachers to

voice the law of love, of spiritual aspiration, of man's divinity, and of his responsibility for his brother man.

Only as in his ruthless struggle he remembers the need for love, can he safely unfold the latent powers of mind, insulated and protected by buddhi, from becoming destructive. It is within a sheath of love that manas must unfold.

To keep the sheath of love active, to rouse in man the principles which will permit him to gain knowledge tinctured by wisdom, the brain guarded and controlled by the heart—this is the work of the spiritual messengers. They teach of man's mission, of his divine origin and of his future heritage. They mark the path in the wilderness of worldly life which will lead out of chaos into attainment and peace.

Lest man, blind and cut away in the turmoil of mind building, lose all memory or understanding of his real mission, the teachers come; lest man be enmeshed by the things of the world, passion and power, they come to hold before him the vision of the goal. Ultimately, he must achieve his Godhood having gained by this arduous journey the jewel of mind. This will put him higher than the angels, not servant only to the law, as the angels who have not yet achieved the power of creative mind still must be, but Master of the Law.

There lies in evolution a nicely adjusted balance; mind to be gained, but not at the cost of spiritual salvation. Is it any marvel that many are lost on the way, that they lose the vision of eternal things in the muck and mire of the fight, and learn to struggle for themselves alone, forgetful of their divine nature, and of the law of sacrifice and of compassion, by which they must at last evolve!

The mind, guarded by impersonal love, can attain divinity and its divine heritage of power. Unless it works within the matrix of buddhi, unless it unfolds within the sheath of unifying love, its intense and separate and destructive activity may tear it away from its higher principles and leave it an isolated unit, robbed of its hope of salvation on this planet.

As said before, throughout the ages the spiritual teachers come to stimulate the activity, first, of those planes of emotion or kama, which are directly linked with compassion or buddhi, and second, through these, of buddhi itself. Until true universal compassion, buddhi, can become active, the sheathing of astral love must enfold the mind.

Therefore, one finds in the older religions marriage required. Through marriage man learns love and personal attachment, and he learns to temper the destructiveness of mind for those he loves and for all dependent things. Marriage is a necessity to evolving man until tenderness is strongly established.

This shows clearly the place of woman in the earlier parts of the scheme. Polarized in kama—emotion and desire— she constantly stimulates emotion in man, and through that, a reflection in buddhi or impersonal love. She is the agent of love during all the earlier cycles, expressing not mind but feeling; holding always as balanced against man's desire for power and conquest, the ideal of the home, of tenderness, of children.

She is the brake upon the wheel of his progress which guards him from himself, which guards him from developing too far the single quality of mind. She reflects for the world the ideal of compassion, of love, of tenderness. Her compassion is often unjust and unwise, but man's justice is often equally unrighteous, seen from the inner vision. It is through the reacting of these mutually irreconcilable forces that the world is safeguarded from manas—mind.

Passion and chivalry are so engrafted in the man as to render him susceptible to woman's influence. The fact that this susceptibility is often used to betray him does not alter the necessity for its existence, for it is the portal to his fortress—the granite citadel of mind—by which may enter that love and tenderness which alone can save him from himself.

As years progress and the cycle turns, man will reach a point where increasing tenderness expresses itself in him, and at that time passion will lose its hold, its purpose fulfilled. Then woman, attaining greater powers of mind, but of an intuitive and abstract type, will complement him on each plane equally, not as now, on alternate planes.

At present man is strongly polarized in the physical and mental more than in the emotional and intuitional as is woman, and thus they supplement one another. In time men and women will develop aspects complementary to one another on all planes, becoming thus far more useful to one another in the work of the world.

The work of the Lords of Compassion has been touched upon before. They send out messengers of light to soften the hardness of men's hearts, and to keep ever before them in the turmoil which is unfolding mind, the underlying law of unity, of love. When the conflict becomes too bitter, then come the messengers again to open the path of love.

This they do, first, to keep the balance of forces. Men must not lose sight of the ultimate goal. Thus will they be protected from falling into the dangers of the extremes of mental arrogance.

Secondly, they come to mark the Path for those who are ready to step out of human evolution into superhuman, to begin to climb the seven steps which lead to divinity. For a point comes in evolution when individual men have attained the necessary development of mind and may graduate from the turmoil and trouble of this world to become "pillars of God who shall go out no more".

They become, then, conscious co-operators and agents for God Himself in carrying out His plans in our world. For these men the Path of Liberation must be clearly defined, and it is they who become the disciples of the teachers, following in their footsteps the law of love, of renunciation and of self conquest.

Thus, we see every great teacher surrounded by a few to whom he teaches the Way of Liberation, the steps which lead to the final unfoldment of spiritual potency. It is they who become the saints of each religion and who carry on the tradition of the Path of Liberation and of Light to future generations.

To those who search deep in the secret annals of any great religion, will appear mention or traces of the teaching which bears upon this Path. In every age, however, of those who seek the Path of Initiation, but few shall find it, and fewer still shall tread it to the end.

But the Path remains ever in existence, and the way may be found by those who bend the energies of their souls to the task. In ancient parlance, it was sometimes called the Philosopher's Stone and those who found it spoke not of it to others.

Today the stress of the world is so great that many souls are ceasing to hope that happiness may be found in the experiences of human life, and are ready, therefore, for the reception of the word of man's purpose in evolution and of the Way to Liberation. For these, then, the qualifications for discipleship are being spoken and the way of attainment thereof unfolded.

CHAPTER II
The Requirements for Discipleship

The requirements for discipleship are—

1. Recognition of the Purpose of Life.
2. Balancing of the Karmic Debt.
3. Orientation to the Path.
4. Study of the Character, weighing of it.
5. Awakening of Compassion to balance Mind.

The first requirement for discipleship is the recognition of the true conditions of worldly life, and the determination to seek something better, to use life here as a stepping-stone to spiritual achievement. This is called the awakening, and until this takes place there is no hope of treading the Path.

The mind must definitely turn away from the hope of personal happiness here and seek the Path. In passing, one should say that the renunciation of earthly happiness does not destroy it. Usually, on the contrary, it brings happiness as a result of the work of the Path. For true happiness comes not from gratified desire but from love and from service for others.

Personal happiness passes. The ones we love die, betray us or leave us, and our solitary way leads but to the grave. Such fragments of personal happiness which are vouchsafed to us are but divine reflections of that universal joy and peace which pulses at the heart of Being. As we teach our personalities here to become instruments of the God within, as we learn to give our love and compassion to a sorrowing world, asking no return, we bring ourselves in touch with this universal joy which pours ever more strongly through us, as we keep the channels open through love and sacrifice.

But the motive of human life must no longer be the search for happiness, but the search for truth. And in this search, sooner or later, the disciple is stripped of all things he holds most dear. In after days these may be given again to him, but only after he has shown that he can go on without them, and that they can never bind him.

For the pilgrim must journey alone, lightly laden. On the Path he may find companions to cheer his way, but he may not turn aside to dally with them, nor leave the Path to succor them if they fall away.

When the disciple sees the world as it is, and definitely turns away from it, this is called the awakening and is the first step in discipleship.

The second is the beginning of the balancing of the karmic sheet. He must study the conditions in which he finds himself, determining as clearly as possible what debts he owes, and what bonds must be broken. He sets himself to making no new bonds, and to equalizing the debts as soon as possible, incurring no new ones, that he may be free for work.

To achieve a clear view of his conditions, his mind must be dispassionate, calm, aloof, and he must see himself, not as a worldly entity surrounded by people and conditions to whom he owes worldly duties, but as a divine spirit come into the world of causes and effects to achieve certain divine purposes of its own.

All things which interfere with the achievement of this purpose must be put aside. Such debts as he feels unavoidable he must pay as rapidly as possible, and realize that the payment must be determined not by the desires and opinions of his friends and family, but by the vision of the divine spirit within him, conscious at last of its mission.

It should be remembered that those who seek to interfere with the fulfillment of this mission, create bad karma; often the disciple, for the sake of those he loves, must not permit them to lay bonds upon him. Nor must he hesitate for one moment as to where his allegiance lies. It can be only to the God within.

Before that transcendent claim all lesser claims fall away. "He that loveth father or mother more than Me, is not worthy of Me." Here the Christ spoke not for Himself, but voiced the cry of that divine spirit within each man, of which He was the expression, that Universal Spirit linked to each human vehicle which sends Its messengers to sound Its call for obedience and for allegiance.

When the balance sheet of karmic debt has been drawn up and the man has oriented himself truly and steadfastly to the goal, he sweeps away within himself all desires that can bind: desires for love, for home, for comfort, for companionship; all those desires which every soul, even upon a worldly mission, must put aside, whether he go to save his nation by war, to aid science by discovery, or to seek the Antarctic pole.

There must be no clinging to personal things. He stands free, having taken the spiritual vow of poverty; poverty not in worldly possessions but in the personal treasures of the soul. Henceforth, one goal alone guides the disciple and dominates his actions—the seeking of the divine within.

This purpose clear, his affairs ordered and organized, the

disciple sets himself to achieve the powers of mind and heart which shall prepare him for his mighty task. Having envisaged his outer conditions, and freed himself mentally and spiritually from all outer personal bondage, he now turns his attention to the character within. which, during many aeons, he has built up. Here, too, must the balance sheet be made of qualities and defects, so that harmony may be achieved in the inner kingdom of the mind and heart, as in the outer life.

In the course of many ages of experience, jewels of the spirit have been acquired, but overlaid many times with dust and rubbish. This rubbish must be cleared away, the jewels polished and cut. The rubbish consists of prejudices, inaccuracies, intolerances, injustices; personal defects, such as impatience, irritation, disorder, slovenliness. These must be steadfastly cleansed away, leaving the jewels of courage, accuracy, patience, tolerance, unselfishness, humility and charity.

The mind awakened, and the outward conditions analyzed, and the debts begun to be paid, the inner conditions analyzed and the work begun upon the rounding out of character, there remains the arousing of the spiritual nature. This means the awakening of compassion for the human race, the recognition of one's essential unity, through God, with man; and responsibility. therefore. to help in man's evolution.

Before the nature is awakened to the purpose of life and to the nature of the goal, the help vouchsafed to the world is of little value. It is unavailing and useless to try to help man upon his way. when one does not know the direction man must travel. Therefore, the first requirement for one who would help, is his own awakening. Once he has definitely visioned the purpose and the Path, he finds enough light to help others upon that Path.

Then must come the recognition that the Path is for all; that the greatest service the disciple renders to man is to tread the Path himself, since each step upon that Path leaves it shining clearer for others! And when he finds his foot upon the Path, when he knows himself firmly established and directed to the goal, he may awaken in others the knowledge he has gained. Since ears are deaf when lulled by happiness, only those can hear who have realized the essential pain of human existence. To those he speaks.

When suffering cuts into the heart, when the personal self lies in fragments, many question the wisdom of the Plan, the benevolence of the Powers which bring worlds into manifestation only, apparently, to suffer and to die. An understanding of the Great Plan alone can restore the sanity of faith. Soon or late, every conscious power, angel or god, must pass through the human kingdom to unfold the powers of mind.

Nature in the worlds here below, offers much to make the way pleasant, yet the purpose of incarnation is not happiness, but the development of mind and of conscious creative power.

In the bitter struggle necessary to attain mind, man is fortunate to have the alleviations he finds in beauty, vigor, companionship, love; for, as said before, the power of mind seems to develop only under the stress of suffering, and of the adverse conditions which make up the greater part of human life.

Mind is needful. The greatest danger to man himself, however, is the development of mind unmodified by love, compassion and tenderness, the qualities of divinity. And at this point, where, among the leaders of the race, mind is reaching high development, it is essential that love and compassion be maintained.

Therefore, today on every side are teachers appearing again

preaching the law of love, messengers from the Wise Guardians in the inner worlds who watch over man's progress on the planet. Some messengers are narrow in their view—the white light of eternal truth rayed through a limited brain; some are universal in their touch; witness the rising of young prophets in so many lands who preach the law of universal brotherhood and of international unity.

Yet the purpose behind remains the same, the need of awakening love and compassion in men and in nations, that at this critical period when mind is strong, it shall be guarded by love from destroying the civilization it has built. Man must achieve divinity, but he may only do so through the guiding of mind by universal compassion.

CHAPTER III

Inner Plane Classes

The spiritual progress of the world is not determined only by the messengers who come to speak spiritual truths in this lower world. People are far more responsive to the truth of spiritual things in the inner worlds which they frequent during sleep; and there, night after night, are classes held by those who desire to help awaken men's souls, and who teach them while they are out of their bodies in sleep, many things which filter through as dim memories or flashes of intuition to the waking consciousness.

Before a man finds in the outer world the light he has been seeking, he has been roused to the search by the things which he has learned on the inner planes.

He has, perhaps, attended one of the great classes or public audiences held by the Wise Ones of the planet, where Their wisdom and radiance is manifest even to the dullest, since their spiritual power is not veiled by the gross sheath of mortal flesh, and eyes are not dimmed by the ignorance and prejudice of the world below.

The work of these classes is carried on by the Masters Themselves, or by high initiates, in order that Their direct influence may arouse the slumbering spark of spirit within those present.

In the classes in the inner planes are given first, the general scheme of evolution and of life, of man's destiny and the method of achievement. When a pupil passes from this class of "hearers" and definitely enrolls himself as a "student", he passes into another group of classes led by chelas, or pupils, for the initial steps of training.

In the outer world he is directed to that literature which embodies the teachings he has been receiving on the inner planes, and which he intuitively recognizes, therefore, as true, and as that for which he has been searching.

When he proves himself to be in earnest in his desire to tread the Path, the greater part of his teaching thereafter will be in the classes on the inner planes. This teaching will filter through in meditation, or in general expansion of consciousness and understanding, especially if he supplements the inner work with persistent reading of books which bear upon the Path of Discipleship.

The first class into which the pupil is directed is that which deals with a study of his own vehicles, especially the three lower ones, mind, emotions and body. His training begins with these three. He is taught to consider himself a divine spirit using for contact with the lower worlds, three instruments, the instruments of action, feeling and thought.

The first work must be done with mind and thought. Until a man thinks rightly, he cannot wisely undertake any training of himself. He is taught, therefore, his relation to the inner worlds, and to this world in particular, seeing the span of life as a training school in which certain faculties and qualities must be gained.

Each incarnation offers new opportunities to carry on the work unfinished, or perhaps marred in the last. If he understands the purpose of incarnation, and awakens to his work early in life, much progress can be made. He must know himself as the true arbiter of his own destiny, and recognize that the conditions in which he finds himself will never improve unless he makes them improve.

The limitations and bonds which he finds here can be broken but by himself, by his own efforts, by a determination to accept as duties only those which his awakened mind holds as such, and to use every available moment of his time in training, study and aspiration.

No human soul is ever wholly free. In every incarnation the necessity for birth, for accepting a family position limits him. Therefore, it is folly to say, "I must wait until I am free." One is never free except as one earns and achieves freedom. A man enters the world bound by associations. Through wise decisions he achieves freedom. This life now is the time to achieve freedom. The power to compel circumstances to yield marks the beginning of growth. Once a man sees that opportunity is now, and determines to seize it, he has taken the first step upward. He has oriented his life to the goal.

The Path of Discipleship requires nice decisions. One must act, if possible, with the greatest detachment. At best one sees but a small portion of the Path. When a man has gained a certain measure of discrimination and adjusted his life with the insight it gives him, he turns his attention to the specific control of his vehicles.

The quality of dispassion and desirelessness must be learned, or rather the desire to attain the goal must draw all other desires into a single Flame of purpose and will. The pupil is taught to control all lesser desires, since they act as bonds upon him. Gradually he must learn indifference to pleasures, permitting nothing to distract him from his major purpose.

This does not mean asceticism, or denial of pleasure as wrong, but it means the gradual indifference as to whether pleasure comes or not, accepting any happiness that comes lightly but avoiding such pleasures as create desires. All self-indulgence must be overcome.

Even after a man has turned his face steadfastly to the goal, there often remain strong desires of a noble type, desires for love, for companionship, for association with those we love. Although love in itself is one form of high spirituality, yet it must not bind; it must pass from intense personal attachment into more intense impersonal tenderness which can even cause the loved one to suffer if it is in accordance with the big plan.

All great achievements are built upon sacrifice, and as a man must put his patriotism to his country before his personal devotion to his wife and family, so a man must put his allegiance to the highest divine law he knows before his personal affections and wishes. It does not mean the sacrifice of the welfare of those one loves. On the contrary those whom we love will profit most by our spiritual achievements for we shall have more to give to them as well as to the world.

But it does mean that all the small obligations and wishes of a personal life must be seen in their true proportion so that jewels of the spirit and high achievements upon the path of divinity may not be thrown lightly aside because of the passing fancies of those who do not understand. Every great achievement the world has ever known has been made possible through sacrifice, sacrifices perhaps unknown and perhaps unrecognized by those close to the one who achieved.

Love must become such that it can bear separation if that, too, is needed. Of all the requirements this is the hardest. Therefore is it said, "Before the disciple can stand in the presence of the Master, his feet must be washed in the blood of the heart." For no man can achieve the goal who does not put the goal, the love of God, above all else.

With this major desire are often minor desires for approval, for appreciation and understanding, for success. Desire for approval in itself is not evil; on the contrary it is good, yet the opinions of others must not swerve the man a hair-breadth from his appointed course nor influence his belief in what is right or wrong for himself.

Lastly, come the desires which find expression in the body: the desire for comfort, for luxury, for food of certain types, for beauty. These, too, are bonds. One must learn complete indifference to the conditions about one. When there is beauty and comfort, enjoy it; when discomfort, forget it. Indifference to bodily comfort is indeed the requirement of every soul who seeks high adventure, whether he be an explorer or a warrior.

So, too, is the detachment from the bondage of personal love, a quality of both warrior and explorer, since only can achievement be made when the personal love is subordinate to the goal in question. Insofar as the love is an inspiration to greater achievement, it is good; but insofar as it acts as a drag upon initiative, it is bondage.

The goal of divinity is indeed a goal of high adventure, for a man ventures all he possesses of worldly happiness, pleasure and comfort, to win the unknown and but dimly visioned prize. So has this world been conquered, by men of strong soul and clear vision, indomitable courage and purpose. So only shall the higher worlds be won, by souls of high purpose and courage, in the greatest of all human adventures, and with the greatest of all rewards for achievement— the winning of Godhood.   It is the supreme adventure.

When man has chosen the Path, has subordinated all desires to this one great purpose, has freed himself mentally from the bonds of personal happiness and comfort, he is ready to attempt the perilous ascent. As an explorer prepares himself by study of the conditions he must face, by learning the language needful, by gaining perfect physical fitness, so the man who seeks the Path, the most dangerous of all adventures, must do likewise.

He must study the available information upon the Way, he must fit himself in mind and body for his task, for this great task of spiritual achievement requires the utmost expenditure of force in every direction, and requires physical, mental and moral fitness in the highest degree. No man who seeks the North Pole can endanger his success by physical indulgence or moral slackness or mental inefficiency.   The price of inefficiency and weakness is death.   In the adventure of all adventures—the discovery of God—inefficiency leads to disaster, despair and madness.

With the recognition of the Way and the method and the training necessary, comes also the need to understand that back of all evolution is fundamental unity, and that unity is love.

One's duty is to achieve the high destiny of mind, but when achieved it adorns not oneself, but, rather, becomes another jewel in the crown of our Solar Lord, for His use and service.   Indeed, we reach our goal at last only by overpowering love for the principle of Goodness and Light, Love and Compassion, which is behind all form.

As a man cognizes and seeks THAT, he comes to have the universal tenderness and compassion which is the mark of spiritual age and maturity. This compassion is not necessarily tenderness to the form in which the spiritual man dwells, that form which often arrogates to itself its divine guest's prerogatives, but to the evolving spirit of man. Compassion fills the awakened man with a passion to free other bound souls and to awaken them to a vision of the goal.

Often man's greatest enemy to his spiritual growth is his personal self, and compassion cannot be shown to the prejudices and peculiarities of that unworthy instrument. Compassion in its truest sense inflicts discipline upon the personality that it may thus relinquish its paralyzing grip upon the soul.

As the Plan unfolds to the awakening spirit, the wonder and beauty of it amazes, and reverence for the patience of the Guiding Spirit, and awe at the courage of Divine Man, flames up. This love and reverence expresses itself in many methods of service and in sincere desire to help man upward.

There are two great motives which lead man to the occult path, to the search for the hidden truth in the universe. One rises from a spiritual distaste for the world, a weariness of soul which makes him long for the eternal; the other, from a great love for humanity and the desire for service. This latter may teach man to renounce the world and all personal desire for the sake of human betterment.

In order to succor the suffering world he will offer all that he has and devote himself to the study of the Path of Wisdom and to achievement upon it, that he may bring light to the world. This is the path of devotion and is the one most easy for women. They, whose great motive power is devotion, service and sacrifice, find in this path the fulfillment of their natures. There are also those souls in masculine bodies who lean to the great Mother side of evolution, and they, too, follow this line.

It is, of all, the safest and surest path, for it lessens the danger of arrogating spiritual power to personal ends, the line of danger, the line of destructive forces, which endangers the soul's link to the body. When the devotion that women have felt for their children is roused by the cry of suffering humanity, and they feel their motherhood for all the sons of men and their responsibility for the race, they will advance rapidly, and through their efforts much will be done for mankind.

Salvation for the race lies in mankind. Only man's help to man can save himself and his brothers. Evil is caused by the evil in man's own heart. Man suffers not from the blows of nature without himself, but from the corrupt and evil civilization which he has built up. Only he can remedy it and build a civilization which is an honor to himself.

In this, woman will help him. After her child bearing period, she has energies and time to devote to the world that men often have not. She has practical experience in keeping harmony, and in meting out justice to a group of individuals. When her wisdom is applied to problems of state much can be learned, much gained.

And because the cycle has turned to the point where many women are developing minds which seek interests beyond their own tiny circle, progress can be made with their assistance. The tremendous mother principle which is theirs by right of their sex, can leaven the lump of suffering, ignorance and crime. It is a cosmic force which, turned to the use of humanity, can achieve miracles.

The first hindrance to progress which must be removed is that which blinds the human mind to the purpose of life.

Material conditions cannot improve until the soul of man is awake and with that awakening he sees his responsibility to other souls. The conditions of civilization which are most lamentable have arisen in the past through the unkindness of man to man. These conditions will be ever renewed until the souls of men awake.

However wisely and skillfully great minds may build civilizations, these civilizations cannot endure so long as there is corruption in men's hearts which will pervert the wisest of forms to serve their selfish purposes. "Seek ye first the kingdom of God, and all these things shall be added unto you." As man becomes spiritually awakened he will save himself and his brothers from the suffering which ignorance and selfishness and indifference have shackled upon the world.

Therefore, this awakening of the soul in others becomes the paramount desire in the man, himself awakened, since through this awakening of the souls of men alone can peace and happiness come upon the earth.

CHAPTER IV

The Battleground

The work of the chela on the probationary path, that path which he enters when he turns his face irrevocably to the goal, is guided by two forces: that of the Teacher or Guide who gives from time to time general instructions and warnings which bear upon the nature of the tests to come, and that of the testing agents or dugpas who are given freedom by the ego to test the personality.

Until the time of probation there are certain magnetic protections about personalities formed partly by the ego, partly by the great groups of spiritual men who throughout the ages have built reservoirs of power for the purpose, and partly by the magic of the esoteric side of religions.

These shells or insulating walls—note the guardian angel summoned by baptism—protect the personality from the assaults of the most destructive elementals of nature. The man is exposed, inevitably, to the changing currents of human moods, anger, lust, greed, cruelty, fear and hatred; but he is safeguarded from the malicious and destructive nature forces by humanity's guardians.

This protection, however, ceases to avail if certain conditions are brought about; first, use of drugs or alcohol in excess, a reason for the greatest care in use of drugs even in operations; second, association with those already obsessed by these entities, as in lunatic asylums and in dens of vice; third, the use of certain occult practices for awakening the kundalini prematurely. This burns out the guardian sheath.

In regard to the second condition, in time it will be recognized that lunatics vary in type. Those possessed of devils should not associate with those whose brains merely have weakened. Also their attendants should be frequently changed. Brutality and cruelty in asylums are largely due to the influence upon the attendants and doctors of the malicious entities surrounding the insane. All lunatics should be given much exercise in the open air and taught to work in the ground. This harmonizes them and brings them in touch with the counteracting nature forces of a constructive kind.

Unless exposed to one of these three dangers, under ordinary conditions man is protected. But when he seeks to become a chela, he is of necessity given some of the tests to prove him fit to become an assistant of the guardians of humanity. He must prove his power not only to resist the attacks upon him, but to control the power of these destructive forces.

Gradually, therefore, the shield is withdrawn and he finds in himself suddenly many qualities of which he had no cognizance, startled into activity by the instrumentality of the dugpas—evil elementals. This is a necessary step.

Yet since fear of the dark forces is dangerous, often the warnings given the chelas are of a general moral nature, because stimulation from the dugpas usually begins to manifest by moral delinquency. If a man truly fulfills his moral obligations as voiced in any of the great religions he cannot fall into serious danger.

A man must know, finally, that all forces, both good and evil, lie within his own nature. These he must control and use. Force uncontrolled falls into vice, yet those forces which gravitate into vice and violence in the early stages of evolution, are just those which make his evolution possible and which give him control, finally, over nature's more constructive forces. "The kingdom of heaven is taken by storm."

Our virtues are negative, our powers positive. These balanced make a man divine. But a chela should not adventure upon the path until his virtues are strong enough to sustain him, as otherwise the increase of power opens the door to the downward way of vice. The path of occultism is strewn with wrecks, verily, since too soon, or too unprepared, man has challenged the destructive forces which he must conquer ere he can tread the Path.

The teachings of the Buddha and of the Christ of gentleness, serenity, virtue, detachment, are the surest safeguards on the Path; and true devotion, unmixed with self, is the safest line of progress. The dugpas cannot trap a selfless man, compassionate, humble and devout. Let man beware of seeking to tread the Path too soon, lest the forces there met awake within him sleeping devils, before he has gained the strength of soul to conquer. Then, in truth, the destructive forces turn and rend, and disaster comes.

During this period of temptation all the forces of nature within man and without him, rise to test his powers of resistance, to test his fortitude and to test his unselfishness. In the history of every great teacher, we find this period described. However great may be the temptations of the world to the ordinary man, they are as nothing compared to the temptations and dangers which beset the man who has challenged the hidden side of nature by seeking conquest on the Path of Initiation.

One should be slow, therefore, to judge too harshly the

apparently disastrous failures of occult students who have dared greatly and not too wisely.

When exposed to the power of destructive forces, the chela becomes the battleground of Kurukshetra in which the forces of the personality, built through ages of combat and selfishness on the involutionary path, struggle with the forces of the spirit, which seeks to master them. It is that this mastery may be complete, that the spirit may prove its power and marshal its forces as rapidly as possible, that the destructive forces are brought to bear upon the personality to awaken in it all latent seeds of good and evil.

The full nature must be brought to maturity, cleansed, purified, and set to service. The force of anger mastered, becomes a titan harnessed. Science is gaining control over the destructive elemental forces of nature; not only controlling destruction, but controlling it by turning that power to useful purposes.

Similarly, the forces within the nature of man which when uncontrolled are dangerous, and, therefore, in the unevolved man are left slumbering as long as possible, in the chela must be roused that he may conquer and control them, and gain thereby his heritage of mastery over nature.

That wrath, which in the uncontrolled man leads to violence, to murder, to cruelty, is the source of power which, wisely directed, gives man control of destructive forces. That power for passion, which in its earlier stages manifests as sensuality, is the strong root buried in the mud which shall flower into divine compassion. That greed, which makes a man gluttonous and selfish, will in time develop the energy of intelligence and forethought which shall bring all nature into subjection.

These three great powers liberate the energy which shall

make him achieve divinity. In their crude form they are destructive, but like fire or electricity or water, when harnessed, they prove man's most dynamic agents for the service of humanity.

Not only do outward circumstances bring difficulties into the life which only courage, coolness and endurance can surmount—friends fail and enemies become peculiarly bitter: but within man's own nature awaken demons of destruction which rise like ghastly spectres of an unholy past.

Man unites within himself both the destructive power of demons and the constructive power of angels. When these two are held subservient to his master will, pledged to the service of God and man, he has gained that conquest of self which makes him a MASTER, and the powers of nature are obedient to his will.

A man is Master not by virtue of his control of elemental forces in nature, not by his feats of magic, not by his powers of vision and prevision, but by his conquest of the forces in his own nature. From the battleground within himself he knows evil and he knows good; he knows temptation and he knows conquest, and he stands steadfast, poised and masterful, directing these forces by his awakened will.

When he has learned to direct wisely these forces within himself, he can likewise direct them in nature. No man can master what he does not understand, and the great atonement of the spiritual teachers comes from the understanding of the sinner's problem. Theirs the power to conquer the force which others still fail to do, and the sharing of strength won in past conflict helps those still prostrate to arise and to assail victoriously the ancient foe.

The tests of the chela are mostly inner ones. Often when the battle is raging most furiously within, outwardly his life may be calm and untroubled. He must learn to lose himself in work, not necessarily world-shaking activities, of which every ardent young soul dreams. but often the daily drudgery which must be glorified by the spirit in which it is done.

Washing dishes becomes a holy thing when done in a spirit of prayer and sacrifice. When we serve man we serve God. Jacob Boehme was a cobbler, yet the glory of his life illumined dark pages in medieval history. The test of the chela is his power to do well, happily, joyously. that task before him. however humble and obscure. Messengers are sent into the world in all ranks of life that the leaven of spiritual wisdom may reach all types of people. Many who could not find the presence of an exalted teacher, are reached by a humble one.

What a man is. determines his worth. not what he does. The mark of the Master is spiritual greatness of soul, not power of mind or success in politics, religion or science. Not by his powers, mental or occult, do we know him, but by his inner majesty of spirit. Magicians of various orders may achieve phenomena and do. Only a noble and masterful spirit can radiate spiritual power.

CHAPTER V
The Chapels of Silence

We have seen that the preliminary training of the pupil is carried on upon the inner planes where he is taught the purpose of life, the vision of the goal and the methods, in a general way, to reach the goal. From the teaching which filters through from the inner planes to his waking consciousness, the pupil or aspirant learns to orient himself in life, so that the goal of liberation dominates his actions.

In him is awakened, likewise, the spirit of compassion, which must guide him safely through the perilous way of the Path. When the spirit of compassion and the desire for service to the world, or service to God, have been fully awakened, when the man has oriented himself to the goal and has adjusted himself mentally, morally and physically, to the accomplishment of his purpose, he passes out of the preliminary classes of the inner planes and enters definitely into a third group of classes, those which teach specifically the training of the vehicles.

The first class planned to awaken the man's spirit to recognition of the laws of evolution and the purpose of life. The second group began his training and taught him the control of the vehicles. The third is open only to those who have proved themselves earnest and dedicated, who have passed the preliminary tests and who have pledged themselves to follow the light at any cost.

In the third group of classes, experimental work is done in dealing with conditions on the inner planes. Usually two years elapse in the preparatory classes before entering the third group. During this preparatory period many fall away. The rest devote themselves to study, to gaining self-control, and to the practice of virtues.

At the end of that time, however, they are held to have sufficient knowledge to permit them to do some work with others already trained, so they are detailed to assist in various groups who are engaged in active work. Among these groups are the invisible helpers who meet newcomers from the earth, and who act as guardians for special souls, pledged to service in the world, and needing, therefore, protection lest some accident cut short their usefulness.

There are groups, too, who try to keep clean and shining certain areas connected with the physical plane, where light from the inner planes can radiate out and where students may gain help and inspiration.

Groups of pupils are divided also according to their need for training. Maps are made of their characters, plotting out their qualities and weaknesses so that they may know themselves. The development of certain qualities is marked out for immediate attention. Then karma is so adjusted as to give them the conditions in which these qualities can be developed most easily; as, for instance, courage or persistence or patience or self-control. Difficulties and problems arise in the outer life which will demand the development of the required quality. If the pupil meets these successfully, he will rapidly achieve the progress desired.

He should, therefore, look upon these difficult conditions as special opportunities vouchsafed to him whereby he can make more rapid progress. It is hard, often, when one is seeking to lead a more spiritual life to find the daily problems sud-

denly intensified. But this intensification marks the attention
of the ego, turned to pressing its personality forward. Difficulties, then, are opportunities, not penalties. If a man can
surmount these difficulties and develop within himself the
powers which will permit him to meet with harmony the
trials of daily life, he will rapidly clear away the obstacles
in the path of his progress. At this point also begins the
special training of disciples for specific types of work.

Upon the inner planes are found the Chapels of Silence,
where echoes of the cosmic song can be heard. It is here that
the interplanetary exchange takes place, where the Lodges in
charge of the planets of our solar system report progress and
exchange greetings.

These Chapels are used for various purposes. They have
about them a magnetic sheath which isolates them from contact with the vibrations of the three worlds, much as De-
vachan, or the heaven world, is isolated from the pain and
suffering of our planet, that wearied souls may rest.

The heaven world is a place of retreat, of joy and refreshment of spirit where those souls who have labored hard in the
physical life may find refreshment before beginning once
more their arduous labors in human incarnation. The heaven
world is a guarded spot protected from all evil and all pain,
established through the compassion of Great Beings in the
earlier days of the history of the planet when conditions on
earth were even more terrible than they are now, and where
only the prospect of future happiness and peace in heaven
made it possible to endure the agonies and cruelties and
anguish of earth life.

The Chapels of Silence are used on special occasions at
specific times as receiving stations for vibrations from other
planets; and chelas are trained to receive these vibrations. At

other times chelas are sent there for meditation. The stillness and isolation from other thought forms permits the bodies to be tranquillized, and the chela can gradually cleanse the vehicles of self-initiated activities, until they become tranquil and limpid.

When this occurs he can in a curious way see into his own vehicles and study their structure, texture, and characteristics or qualities, and so learn much about himself and his own problem. He begins to know himself and to see the plan of his evolution. It is similar to what the ego achieves at death.

Structure means the basic type of response to vibration in the vehicles. Texture means the fineness or coarseness of the matter drawn into them. Quality or character means the varying powers of mind and emotion built in by the virtues and vices.

In the Chapels of Silence one learns to see himself as he truly is. Every man has a fundamental response to life which is his keynote, the keystone of his arch, determined by his ray and sub-ray. First he discovers whether he is interested in the form and the building of the form, or in the thought which lies behind and ensouls the form.

This is a very fundamental difference which continues up to the Godhead itself. In all nature, in all of evolution there are the two great forces at work; one shaping the form, one unfolding the spirit, and these two working together are the secret of all manifestation and of all progression.

Every man must be allied to one side or the other in his final analysis. All artists, all gardeners, all surgeons and many doctors, all builders respond to the building of form. All teachers, spiritual and clerical, most political leaders, writers, philosophers, scientists, soldiers, respond to the spur of spirit or mind.

The structure may differ also in this way. One man may interpret all things in terms of color, another of sound, another of form; one may be geometric in his thought forms, another create more indefinite flashes of light, another may link up rather with human feelings and characteristics and interpret vibrations in terms of man. Another may interpret in terms of nature, akin to the spirit expressed in mountains, trees, fields. As was said it is determined by the sub-ray or sub-plane to which a man has attuned himself.

In these Chapels of Silence the disciple slowly begins to see himself as if reflected in a mirror. He learns the keynote of each vehicle, first of the three lower belonging to the personality, body, emotions and mind.

Frequently each vehicle manifests a different one of the three gunas or attributes, as activity, rhythm and stability. Some have activity of the body; some, activity of the emotions: some. activity of the mind. Some have activity of all three. In other cases the dominant quality of the dominant vehicle shadows or reflects itself in the other two.

Usually, intense mental activity of the lower mind manifests as restlessness in the physical body—uncontrolled activity in the mind, that is, not slow, sequential reasoning. Activity in the emotional body also shows itself in action, but rather in impulsive actions and in the need for excitement, than in restless physical activity. This is often a failing of women.

Rhythmic vibration in the lower vehicles makes a pleasant vibration for all near that person, but it often means lack of power in the mind. It brings instability and indecision. If, however, intuition is aroused, this may be active and accurate.

In any case, the disciple is not desired to change the type of activity, but rather to develop its highest qualities, control and apply them. Slowness of mind serves concentration and continued effort. The mind does not tire easily, and makes the deep student. Swiftness of mind brings alertness and action in emergencies—the executive. Rhythm brings justice but often indecision. Stability in the vehicles often reflects itself as stubbornness and obstinacy, and the inability to learn quickly. But it means endurance, steadfastness and, usually, loyalty. In each case a balancing point must be sought where the best qualities of the type of vehicle are used and counterbalanced.

It must be clearly understood that the three gunas, action, stability and rhythm, are manifestations of three types of force which exist in the universe, no one of which can be said to be better than the other; they are merely different with different uses and qualities.

Rajas or action can be likened in the physical world to electricity; inertia or stability to the unmoving strength of the mountains; and rhythm to the ceaseless movement of the sea. Often rhythm is interpreted as harmony. It is in actuality only the intermediate balancing force of the three.

Then, too, a man must learn to know the dominant force in himself. Action, will, and desire or intelligence. The main source of motive is kama manas, mind colored by desire; ambition and love being the two common forces, masculine and feminine, and almost equally selfish.

These manifest themselves in the three vehicles. Ambition in the physical manifests as ambition for physical power; in the astral or emotional, as ambition for domination over others—one pole of cruelty; in the mind, as ambition for conquest in the mental world.

Love manifests, first, in the physical body as sensual indulgence; second, in the astral as an intense sex nature, a constant demand for attention; third, in the mental as desire to feel one's sex power over men or women regardless of the pain inflicted. Here the dominant note is astral—sex desire. These are, of course, the low types of the forces.

These two great forces, love and ambition, replicas of buddhi and manas, negative and positive, manifest, modified, however, by the types of matter in which they work on each plane.

As the student learns to know himself, as he learns his tools, he learns also what qualities he needs to protect him from the shadow of his powers. And these he seeks to unfold. Activity needs poise and tenderness, it being violent and destructive. Inertia or stability needs energy roused by the motive of devotion. Rhythm needs steadfastness, perseverance. Each ray and sub-ray has its compensating ray or quality which must be developed to establish balance.

It is the purpose of the teachers to teach each man to know himself; to know his type, his way or line of evolution and his strength and weakness. The purpose is not to change the type but to develop it to the highest point of efficiency.

To do this the powers peculiar to his ray must be unfolded, and at the same time the necessary safeguards to the dangers of that ray built in, so that a man may become through his training, efficient, balanced and dependable.

When the disciple has entered the preliminary classes, and passed through the preliminary training outlined, so that he has begun to gain some control over his vehicles, he is taken night after night to special magnetized parts of the inner worlds where forces can be played upon him which will result in definite stimulation of certain of the vehicles.

After the disciple has learned somewhat about himself and has made the first steps in the knowledge of the Self, in the preliminary classes and in the Chapels of Silence, he is given into the charge of a chela who carries out a program laid down by one of the Masters, receiving the disciple each night and accompanying him on his pilgrimage to the centres allotted for that night.

In this way the disciple or pupil visits some of the museums where replicas of ancient ceremonies are on view, in order to stimulate again in him memories of forces and truths gained in earlier lives. Usually a pupil comes into Theosophy because of a memory that has been aroused of some past life which marked occult progress for him. One of the surest ways of holding him to the Path is to permit that occult memory to be vivified and the atoms responsive to it stimulated. Flashes of the past then come in waking consciousness, as feelings, thoughts, even as pictures.

It has the effect often, however, of causing the pupil to choose out of the present teaching only that which is similar to the work and outlook of the past. This is dangerous, as in each age, owing to the magnetic polarity of the period and the change in the forces playing about the earth's surface and through the races of men, new methods must be used. The forces must be handled differently. The polarity and construction of men's bodies differs in each age and race, and likewise the forces differ which are available for use. One must adapt oneself to the new age.

After the old memories are well aroused, sometimes of more than one life, lives in Egypt, India, Persia, wherever the Light was dominant and the occult teaching available, the disciple is given the opportunity to try to awaken some of the powers and knowledge he had of old. Sometimes this is most successful and the inner worlds begin to open up to the waking consciousness in a way to give confidence to the man.

These early experiences, however, should not be given too much weight. They are but broken memories which are vivified in order to assure the waking consciousness of the reality of the inner worlds. True vision comes later; vision of work now on hand or to be attained in the future. The fragments of the past must not establish ancient habits of thought and feeling which would not be suitable to the present unfoldment.

The next step is the establishment of certain qualities in the character which balance vices; for anger, tenderness; for sloth, passionate devotion: for selfishness. compassion.

When the pupil has gained knowledge of himself and of his needs, he is shown the three paths of action, wisdom and will. Action or karma takes him finally into the class called the Masters, whether upon this planet or another, who are the direct agents of the Law upon each planet. Wisdom takes him into the Nirmanakaya class, working with the spirit of things, the forces which play upon all evolving life.

The Nirmanakayas fill the reservoirs which supply spiritual forces to the world and upon which the Members of the White Lodge and Their chosen instruments may call for the benefit of man and of the planet. They control the magnetic currents about the earth.

The third path, that of will, is one rarely chosen. It has to do with the work of the Kumaras, Who are the Guardians of the powers of the planet, and Who are the Arbiters of the destinies of nations and of continents. They become the ultimate judges of good and of evil, the holders of the keys of power whereby destruction is loosed upon the planet when the nice balance between good and evil, which is necessary to evolution, becomes endangered by the over balance of evil.

At such times they loose upon the planet those forces which

result in cataclysms, and which destroy the evil centres on the
earth. They have in Their hands the carrying out of the de-
crees of doom. They control the destructive forces in the
universe and loose them when need arises.

CHAPTER VI

The Tests of the Probationary Path

A chela's advance is determined by the rapidity with which he can meet and conquer the forces of his nature, and by the speed with which the destructive, elemental forces of the planet may safely be loosed upon him.

Usually the first onslaught is the most destructive. If he passes and conquers this, he progresses rapidly. If, however, the defeat is not complete, the test is made again and again through the years until a man feels he is beset by furies, as indeed he is.

The greatest test is usually doubt. For if doubt can be cast upon the truth of evolution and upon the reality of the Path, the very strength of a man's will is nullified. There is no power to fight.

The next greatest test is personal love. When a man turns his face to the solitary Path of Discipleship, he must leave behind in spirit, the mortal ties which bind him to earth. Not less dear are the loved ones, but for their sake as for his own, must he loose the bonds upon his soul which bind him to the ways of earth. Not that he must leave those he loves, but that he must cease to lean upon them or to centre his life about them.

The focus of interest must change, and the one dominating purpose of life, the fulfillment to the uttermost of the Law, must order his thought. More tender will he be, more unselfish in his love, since now he gives all and seeks nothing. It is the change of the inner point of view that matters; the orientation to God. No longer are his loved ones, his. They are but servants and children of God, whom it is his privilege to love and to serve, but to whom he may not cling, nor for whom may he grieve, if the plan requires that they pass to other work.

This is the spiritual meaning of the vow of poverty. A man may hold millions in his control and yet be poor in spirit, in that his life and all he has are dedicated to the service of the world and held in trust for God.

The third test is that of anger or hatred. The disciple must learn to receive injustice, slander, betrayal, without anger or hatred. It is not his concern what others may do to him. The Law will bring justice on all points. But what matters is whether onslaughts by destructive forces through human agents can stir destructive forces within him. Not the attitude of others to him, but his to all the world, determines his progress.

Indeed, insult, injury, treachery, are necessary steps in the occult life to prove a chela's character and strength. Hence, all spiritual teachers, great and small, are beset by traitors, false friends and vindictive enemies, even such as Judas, in the story of Jesus. Judas is not only a historical person but a symbol of a universal truth. In a sense a man's enemies are his best teachers, since they offer the tests which alone can assure his spiritual unfoldment. Suffering is the price of progress.

The point of view of the occult student upon the probationary path must of necessity differ somewhat from that of the average person of the world. When he first places his foot upon that narrow Way which leads to Initiation, of his own free will he challenges fate and demands from the gods the priceless gift of discipline.

This discipline must make of him not only a kindly and a good man, but a wise man, a powerful man, and above all, a man who has been tested in every way for human weaknesses, and conquered.

This does not mean that when a man becomes an Initiate he will be free from human weaknesses. On the contrary, they may, some of them, be intensified; but it does mean that he has shown powers of stability, forbearance, compassion, and desire for service to the world which prove him, probably, strong enough to resist some of the major temptations later on the way.

Perhaps the hardest test that has to be passed successfully is this test of hatred and malice. A man must prove that neither injustice nor cruelty nor unkindness nor betrayal can rouse in him the desire for vengeance; must prove that he is free from the terrible dangers of hatred. He may be hurt, he may be angry, he may feel injustice, but he must accept these without hatred.

It is necessary to change one's point of view; to expect not justice but tests. A man must meet disappointment and betrayal, actual or seeming. He may meet all these things perhaps from those he loves most. It may be in fact, it may be only in seeming, but the test must be met and must be passed. In the end the Akashic Records show the truth and he will be judged accurately to the last tiny act. We may all rely upon that law to bring us full justice.

Therefore, it matters not if we seem unjustly treated; it matters only whether we be just to others. When conditions are hard and when comrades fail, love betrays and friendship falters, let us look upon it as a testing necessary before we may feel our feet firmly planted upon that upward way which leads to Liberation. Until we have been tried to the uttermost we cannot know our own strength, nor can those Wise Guardians of humanity depend upon us to help Them in Their great task.

Therefore, when we meet injustice, let us bear no resentment to those who so act, but laugh and recognize it as a clever test of the gods, which we have demanded. It is sometimes hard to remember this when suffering the indignities of persecution, but it is nevertheless an inevitable part of the Path and these tests may be more lightly and surely passed if one learns to avoid self-pity and to look upon hardships as opportunities and not as penalties.

In the long distant future, when we look back from the heights of Adeptship upon the trials of the personality, we shall realize that the greatest opportunities of progress were given us not by our friends, but by those who seemed our enemies, who, by their apparent injustice and cruelty gave us the opportunity to pass the tests required by the upward Path of Initiation.

During the training and testing of the disciple on the probationary path, his progress is watched and recorded by a Master or by a high chela. The sum of efforts, of failures and of successes is recorded. and according to the balance of these, is increased force given. Those who have earned by dedication in past lives and by renewed efforts in this, the power to hear the Master's voice, are given, from time to time in meditation, counsel, admonitions or encouragement.

The disciple must be tested; such is the Law. But the Teachers watch with hope, almost prayerfully, his ascending steps. Every successful disciple who treads the Path to the Portal of Initiation, marks a reward to the Teachers' age-long labors, and lightens the load of Their responsibility.

No one could be more tender, more solicitous, more eager for the success of a pupil than these Elder Brothers, Who have pledged Their lives to the service of man, incarnation after incarnation. Yet in the crucial hour of test for which the pupil has been prepared with counsel and training, They must stand aside and let the test prove the disciple's own strength and intuition.

As in the world, the teacher may not help or counsel the pupil during an examination, so may not the Master guide the blinded steps of the disciple during the hours of test. The disciple must prove his own strength alone, his steadfastness, wisdom and intuition, under the assaults of blindness, destructive anger, hatred, ambition and doubt.

When a pupil has definitely sought the probationary Path and turned his face to the goal of divinity, when he has proved his earnestness and dedication, he is allowed to draw upon the Master's forces for inspiration, strength and encouragement. As he reaches upward with love and aspiration the Master pours out His strength to help the disciple.

But when the hour of test is come, the Master withdraws His aid, that the inner strength of the disciple be proved. If the pupil reach the Master then, it must be by his own unaided efforts that he break through the barriers of the destructive forces which have been permitted to come about him. This is the test or series of tests.

Can he break through the mists which surround and blind him and progress upward into the eternal Light? If he can, then does he find the Light shining within himself—the true Light which he seeks and which alone can illumine the Path as he passes onward. Each time that he breaks through the mists of illusion thrown about him, the Light within leaps up and increases its steady glow. Another facet of the divine jewel has been polished, to remain ever as a testimony of man's divine heritage.

As the chela passes successfully the tests, as he proves his capacity to stand alone, to follow the Vision, to find the Light within, he begins to be drawn closer to the Master and to share in His work.

More power is made available for the chela's use, since it has been proved that he can be trusted to react well to its stimulation. He begins to enter upon his period of service in which he distributes the Master's force, or more accurately, a small portion of the force of the White Lodge, either in active service in the outer world, or in intimate contact with those about him.

The use of this force expands and develops his vehicles and their powers. His brain increases in power, his devotion in intensity and purity, his actions in accuracy, skill and force. Moreover, he becomes more radiant, a luminous, serene and joyous figure in the dark atmosphere of worldly life.

At the same time he begins definite training on the inner planes in which he is taught the use and the control of forces there. Little by little he gains knowledge of the control of the various elements, of the elementals connected with them, and of the devas in charge of the elementals.

In all these things he is taught how to command the services of deva and of elemental, in the name and by the authority of the White Lodge, as an agent of Its Power. He must not by purchase, by bribe, gift or tribute, gain the services of these forces as many lesser ones do, to attain a modicum of magical power. He is taught the line of evolution of these elementals, the motive power of their action, and the type of force which they obey. This differs for different elementals and devas. To accomplish this control, three things are needed:

1st: Serene courage, which has no element of doubt or fear as to the power to control.

2nd: Absolute dedication in the use of the forces, using them only for the work, not for oneself, or for the pleasure, even, of using them.

3rd: Serenity. Irritation and anger endanger the use of these forces. It disturbs the elementals and may cause them to turn and attack the one who commands them. It is similar to handling a swarm of bees. Courage, serenity and dedication are essential.

Many fail, because in handling the elementals they lose control of themselves, and are, therefore, attacked by the forces they use; much as an electrical engineer might endanger himself, if in a fit of irritation he jammed up the machinery controlling the currents of high voltage.

When the chela has proved himself fit for advancement by carrying the Master's force successfully, and by resisting the attacks, and surmounting the tests, he passes to the point of becoming an accepted disciple.

This means that he will have access to the reservoirs of the Master's powers at any time to use for the helping of the work. He will then begin definitely to find the force he needs for service. While on probation, he has found at times a downpour of force to meet some especial need. Now he can summon it at will.

When the pupil has passed the tests of the probationary Path and has become accepted by the Master, Who will train and guide him, the Portal of Initiation opens before him. Beyond this Portal lie the shining peaks of achievement which shall lead him ultimately to God, and to his heritage as a Son of God.

PART III
The Accepted Disciple

CHAPTER VII
Departments of the Hierarchy

The work of the accepted disciple differs from that of the probationer. He has already power to control circumstances so as to orient his life to the occult laws. He has taken his character in hand and to some extent trained and educated and co-ordinated it, and he has shown some capacity for service in the world.

He is considered fit, therefore, for special training, which shall prepare him safely to handle certain occult forces on the inner planes, and to transmit those forces in part at least, through his lower vehicles to the world of man.

There are two great ways of service among Adepts. One demands work principally on the physical plane, actual work among men, either in giving spiritual light to their minds directly as a teacher; or by organizing channels such as churches or schools; or by actually sharing in the reform work politically and socially which is going on in the world.

The other way consists of work, entirely or almost so, upon the inner planes; the building of reservoirs, the stimulation of occult centres, the manipulating of magnetic currents and other planetary forces: the directing of forces in nature which affect climatic conditions and change the form of continents.

To some extent both kinds of service are required of the chela. The proportion of inner and outer plane work depends upon what his future is to be when he reaches the Adept level. If he is going to become a Master, that is, one who works directly with members of the human race, a large part of his work as a disciple will be with men upon the physical plane.

The work of an Adept who becomes a Master is quite different from that of one who does not. A Master has a direct relationship with men; in fact, he is called Master because he takes pupils. He may hold official positions in the Hierarchy with regard to man such as Manu, Bodhisattva and Mahachohan, or become one of the Officials of the Seven Rays; or he may share in the occult social structure, serving in one of the departments for the supervision and guidance of the race. These work primarily with men, with the consciousness of humans, and their social and political forms, and with the forces playing through humanity.

The work of each Manu, of course, includes besides the work with humanity, the establishing of a continent which shall be suitable in climate, flora, fauna and food, as well as magnetic conditions, for the development of the peculiar traits and characteristics which His people must manifest.

But this work is only undertaken after He has reached a very high level, and consists in laying down the plans and specifications which must be followed by the nature workers and the builders of organic and inorganic forms, rather than the manipulation of the forces themselves.

When the time arrives for His work, He summons from the occult laboratories hundreds of specialists who have been experimenting along the lines of continent building for thousands of years, and into their hands places much of the responsibility for the carrying out of the plans. His major work consists in hammering masses of men into shape.

By playing one group against another socially and politically, the right balance of the nations under His control is kept; by contest and by struggle, as well as by peace and prosperity and the various arts which follow therefrom. He must develop certain qualities in His peoples according to the Plan laid down for Him by the Ruler of the Planet, and according to the Plan laid down for the Ruler of the Planet by the Archetypal Logos, Who supervises planets of a certain type and bent of evolution in a given group of solar systems.

For although our Logos is in direct charge of His own Solar System, He invokes the aid of other high Logoi Who have specialized in certain types of evolution in the past, and Who are, as it were, Advisory Experts to the various Logoi in relation to difficult parts of the solar evolution. All this has to do with the manifested side of evolution on the physical plane.

A Manu is undoubtedly a great occultist, but one primarily Who knows where to enlist the services He needs and to requisition the knowledge necessary for the building of His kingdom. Whereas kings rule over one kingdom for a lifetime, made up often of various states, all subordinate to their authority, the Manu's kingdom covers the birth and growth of a great Root Race, and includes many civilizations, nations and empires within it. Nevertheless, there is a close similarity between the duty and functions of the ruler of an empire and those of a Manu.

Those Initiates who work to bring about the form side of evolution usually become Masters, often heads of the department under the Manus, and ready to take pupils either to prepare them for given work under the Manu, or for the particular work of the department in which the Masters Themselves are active.

Included under the department of the Manu and race build-

ing are the departments of the Bodhisattva and the Mahachohan, with all their various ramifications. All this is primarily
work in the world of man and with the various forces, elemental and otherwise, working through man and the kingdoms associated with man.

But there is another great line of evolution which works
primarily with the inner forces. It is closely associated with
the work of the devas, and the Adept who follows it nearly
approximates some of their work. It deals not only with the
building of great reservoirs for the storing of power, magnetic,
spiritual and elemental, but it includes the actual development
of the forces of nature on the inner and outer planes, latent in
matter.

Chelas who are destined for this kind of inner plane work
when they reach the Adept level, begin at once their training
in the handling of occult forces. These forces are quite different from the forces used by humanity and dedicated to its
service. They are related rather to the evolution of the planet
itself and to the opening up of occult centres in the Planetary
Body.

This department deals with many strange and mysterious
things, forces not only emanating from the great Power
House in the centre of the earth, but from the various sheaths
which make up the physical, etheric, emotional and mental
bodies of the planet.

In such sheaths are certain forces latent which must gradually be evolved and unfolded so that planetary growth may
be harmonious and balanced. Those who work with these
forces more nearly approximate, in the Planetary Body, the
cells in the body and brain which control the subconscious
in physical man.

Also, however, chelas on this line must learn to summon

from the solar system and the whole Cosmic System, special forces for use as need arises, much as the etheric body learns unconsciously to draw prana or vitality for the body's use. Only in the large planetary plan the cells and centres represented in man by the subconscious are represented by conscious Entities Who direct this work.

Also the chelas experiment in learning to contact new inter-solar forces and make themselves foci whereby these forces can be distributed to the planet. There are many strange things in this connection, still unknown to most of us. We touch but the fringe of that other consciousness, the subconscious, even in our own body, and much less so in the Planetary Body.

Entities are brought over from time to time from other regions and other solar systems to instruct the planet and to help invoke some unusual and hitherto unattainable forces. Then, slowly and with great caution, this second department of Adepts and Their assistants learn to develop in themselves conditions and vibrations which will permit them to transmit these forces for the planet.

Occasionally, too, there are strange invasions and incursions from errant groups of destructive agents, either arriving here by chance, or brought here to give the planetary workers certain tests and trials. Great, then, are the calls for rapid action on the part of the Guardian Group in the Hierarchy.

There are many evolutions carried on in the planet which have little or no relation to man. Humanity might be said perhaps to correspond to one group of cells in the planetary body, with one major function, perhaps the cerebro-spinal in certain aspects.

But there are many others whose existence we either do not recognize or cannot understand. After all, the evolution of man is only incidental to the evolution of the planet. Man profits by sharing in that evolution, but it is not primarily for his benefit that it exists. Elemental essence profits by being used by man for his own purposes of evolution, but it does not exist primarily for him: it is but one of the materials included in a vaster plan available for his temporary use.

So man's life and growth upon this planet contributes some necessary element to the planetary growth, and through sharing in this growth and contributing these necessary elements to the intricate planetary life, he is permitted thereby to profit through experience and through evolution, for himself.

It is to his advantage to shorten his stay in this particular stage as much as possible. He contributes to the well-being of the planetary evolution most by hastening through it as rapidly as possible, and by not delaying his growth or seeking to turn the forces too much to his own uses. For his evolution hastens all evolution.

It is his duty, very much like a cell in the body, to help carry on the Planetary life, to fulfill his functions here, and to make his contribution to the magnetic forces of the planetary body. His happiness and his well-being are dependent upon his fulfilling this required service. All other pleasure or happiness is incidental, and destroyed if it clashes in any way with the requirement of service.

A man who attempts to seize personal happiness or personal power at variance with this law of service to the planet, becomes like a cancerous group of cells in the body, which are at war with the needs of the whole body. He or his group, if they become powerful enough to endanger the life of the whole, are cut out and destroyed, if they cannot be re-oriented to their duty.

It is this which happens in the periodical Days of Judgment, an example of which we have in the destruction of Atlantis and in the aeonic damnation of which the Christ warned men in the Bible.

It is this need to fulfill a required service to the planet which is the basis of the teaching of dharma. It is inevitable at this stage that men should seek personal happiness, but it is obtainable only as the result of the fulfilling of dharma—duty; service to the plan. All religions teach the duty to God as the first requisite. The great teachers sought to put in simple form this law of the required service to the Planetary Logos, to teach man not to seek happiness in personal satisfaction.

Happiness comes only in the carrying out of the plan, and those are happiest who base their happiness upon the plan, and not upon other humans. If humanity could once grasp the relation between happiness and this fulfillment of service, many grief-stricken hearts whose lives seem broken and useless would be at peace.

By living, just by living nobly, they serve the Law. Suicide in most cases is a sin against this fundamental law of obedience to and service to the Planetary Spirit. It is a soldier who falters in the great campaign.

CHAPTER VIII
Occult Forces

The accepted chela becomes an outpost of the consciousness of his Master. In other words he begins to be called upon to distribute on the physical plane some of the forces the Master has at His command. This requires a certain sensitizing of the body in order to temper it, to make it responsive. The nerves must be tensed, like keying up a violin.

There are several methods of doing this. One is to live in a highly magnetized spot or in close contact with the Master. Another is intensity of joy and pain, either physical or emotional or mental or all three. However, as occult steps always require the paying of certain karma—debts—usually there is a clever adjustment made so that the debts are paid, and the suffering involved at once develops the necessary qualities in the character, and sensitizes the nervous system.

As rapidly as possible the Master starts pouring force through his chela. As rapidly as possible also the chela learns on the inner planes to manipulate the forces necessary for his inner plane work. Little by little he is exposed to the impact of different elemental currents from which the average man is protected, until the chela proves himself able to meet these forces without wavering in any vehicle.

This is not as easy as it sounds. There are not only the primary elemental forces connected directly with man and playing through him for his development and evolution.

These in themselves are powerful enough, as can be seen where uneducated groups are subjected to emotional impacts and mob psychology results, but there are greater currents which are not particularly related to man and which belong either to other evolutions, or to the life proper of the Planetary Spirit, which man occasionally contacts by chance.

The force is stupendous, literally an inner world cyclone or high voltage power current. Many chelas, especially those who are to do outer plane work and to become ultimately the guides and teachers of humanity, are required to understand only the human forces and those distributed on the planet for use and help of man and his related kingdoms. Sometimes these chelas are said to belong to the branch who take Initiation under the Planetary Group.

But playing through the planet are other forces which belong rather to the solar system and even the inter-solar scheme. These are present for the development of the planet itself, and those consciousnesses on the planet who are linked to the Inter-solar Group.

These forces are directed to the planet from vast distances and from centres entirely outside of our present solar system. They are part of the inter-cosmic forces which are playing on our solar system as a whole for the evolution of our Logos and His chief associates.

Groups of His associates are established in the various planets partly to help His work, partly to carry on Their studies and Their own development, through experience in administering these forces for the system and for the planet. These are the Kumaras of planets and Their associates Who form the Inner Council of Power.

Among those who achieve Initiation there are a few who seek to qualify ultimately for this special group, and who take the training required. These are required at each Initiation not only to pass the tests in the ordinary planetary forces, but also in the solar and inter-solar forces. A peculiar quality of will is required for this, and the manipulation in special ways of the elemental forces of fire, air, water and earth, so as to learn to charge the inner vehicles in such a way that they can endure the play of the greater forces without being rent asunder; and also to form a protecting shell about the physical body, so that the residue of force in the inner vehicles after experimentation will not cause too severe a repercussion upon the physical when the sleeper awakes.

The chelas on this line work primarily with the forces of one or other of the four elements, earth, air, fire and water, become experts as it were in one department. The earth magic is really planetary magic, and more or less available to all Initiates. But water magic is very potent, being one of the two primary creative elements, the other being fire.

Air is an offshoot of fire, as earth is of water. Air offers control of the forces of the planets of the solar system. Water enters into the ocean of space and gives access to inter-solar forces. Fire represents kundalini, creative power loosed in atomic motion, and gives access to almost all occult forces in the inter-solar scheme. The interplay of these two, fire and water, brings about all manifestation.

In the deva kingdom also, there are divisions between those handling planetary and those manipulating inter-solar forces, one of which leads to the position of Chief Administrator of the Solar Forces, and Director of the Inter-cosmic Currents. The devas have great responsibility as to the amount of force they summon from the solar system for the use of the planet; wisely to judge of this, and wisely to distribute it so that the harmonious relation of different parts of the planet and the evolving kingdoms on the planet will persist.

Much of their energy latterly has been given to counter-balancing as skilfully as possible the destructive forces that man has been loosing during the past five thousand years while he was passing through his period of unconscious darkness. Previous to this he co-operated with the devas either consciously or in obedience to religious laws laid down by wise teachers.

When Kali-Yuga began, however, this general co-operation ceased. All over the planet the positive and dynamic occult centres were sealed to prevent the outpouring of force which would increase man's destructiveness, and which, when closed, greatly diminished his power. One reason for the great increase in disease during that period is due to the diminished vitality in man from the closing of these active centres in the world.

Thus, the work of keeping the world well-balanced and tolerably clean devolved upon the devas alone, with a few rare exceptions among souls of transparent vision able to know the law and to co-operate. The religions became rationalistic or devout instead of being instructed, scientific and magical.

Only the negative reservoirs tapped by devotion, love, aspiration, and self-abnegation, were left available to man, since these could not easily be misused by man to his own destruction during his period of ignorance and darkness.

CHAPTER IX

The Work of the Different Masters

As the accepted disciple begins to handle the forces on the inner planes, the play of forces through the vehicles does two things. Because it unfolds the latent powers in him much more rapidly than in the average man, as the steady playing of warmth in a hothouse intensifies the growth of a plant, there are two results.

First, the play of force increases the vigor with which both virtues and vices manifest, and intensifies the man's struggle with himself; secondly, this speeding up of the unfoldment of the latent powers also automatically speeds up the rate at which a man lives, so that he passes in a few years through the experience of a lifetime, and in those few years lives through the karma of a lifetime. In this way he speeds up very greatly the precipitation of karma, both good and bad.

The accepted disciple has definitely set out to achieve his goal—the unfoldment of divine powers within himself up to the point required by evolution on this planet—as rapidly as possible, and far more rapidly than the average man. He has pledged himself to endure the penalties exacted by that speed in achievement, which are very great, physically, morally, and mentally; and he has pledged himself to use the powers as they unfold for the service of the world.

Calmness is the great requisite under the tension of expanding vehicles. The tests are given in different order, but some of them include tests in patience, pride. anger. conceit. fanaticism. detachment. There must be calmness of mind, of body, of emotion; there must be regularity of life, a definite pressure maintained upon the vehicles to control them and develop their powers harmoniously.

Excitement, restlessness, desire for results, passion. pride. depression. all are stumbling blocks, which must be overcome. There must be a calm dispassionate purpose to build up gradually the qualities and vehicles required, day by day, month by month; and the desire to work at once before training is accomplished, to see results, often defeats the purpose.

The training is the first step. Can an engineer be trusted to build until he has finished his training? This applies, however, only after one is on probation and under training. Earlier, the act of service proves a man's fitness for probation.

The first Initiation marks the point where the Master considers that the pupil is able to receive successfully the forces up to a certain voltage, and has proved his capacity to turn this increased force to service; in other words, he has reached the point where he can be permitted to enter as an independent member into that Brotherhood which *distributes* the forces governing the growth of the planet, and has proved sufficiently trustworthy to have access to the reservoirs available for that Body.

When he has passed the fifth Initiation he enters that Group who have to do with the *administering* of the forces of the planet, and the establishing of reservoirs for the distribution of the Brotherhood. This Group has the responsibility of gathering into the planet from the solar system the forces They consider necessary for use in a given period. and the allocation of those forces to the various departments, much as a government allots its budget.

The work of the accepted disciple is to prepare himself as rapidly as possible to take his place in the Brotherhood, and this is done by the triple action of controlling vehicles so that they can handle the forces on the outer planes, of learning to handle the forces on the inner planes, and of handling his bodies under the repeated impacts of karma coincident with his growth.

In fact, the development of the disciple depends upon the growth in him of strength, steadfastness and unselfishness; strength coming from the increased power in handling forces; steadfastness in the unshaken front with which he meets the problems within himself and in his life precipitated by karma: and unselfishness in the increasing capacity to turn all his powers to the service of the world.

His intelligence and discrimination must, at the same time, be constantly developing so that he will learn wisely to use the force at his disposal. Just as a rich man must learn wisely to administer his money, so the occult student must learn wisely to allocate his time, his strength and his service. The world is not served by the indiscriminate giving of money to all who ask it. The administrator of public or private funds soon learns that to answer all appeals for money quite often does more harm than good.

In the same way, the work of the world is not profited by sympathy which permits one to become as it were a moral post upon which others lean. Every mother knows that if she loves her children wisely she will not grant all their requests, and that the fibre of manhood is not built by over-indulgence, or by too much sympathy. Encouragement, yes, and the strengthening of their wills, but not an endless listening to the babble of self-pity, and certainly not an attempt to prevent their meeting the consequences of their mistakes.

There has been a misunderstanding in the world as to the meaning of a spiritual teacher. To some the Christ was a Comforter. But to some He was a Flail of Righteousness, a retribution for their evil deeds. To some He gave pity and aid, but to some He gave tasks beyond their power to achieve, as in the case of a young man having great riches.

Men perhaps at times need comforting, but most of all they need assurance as to the goal, and leadership in courage, in independence, and in sacrifice of worldly considerations to attempt that goal. For the Great Teachers come not so much to comfort us for our sorrows, as to mark out the route of conquest whereby we may enter the new worlds. It takes supreme courage and supreme strength to storm the gates of the Kingdom of God.

All who achieve Initiation, however, are not on their way to the attainment of Christhood or Buddhahood. This is one office among many, and requires peculiar qualifications which only the exceptional man, even among the Brotherhood, can achieve.

When a Christ enters upon His Great Office, His compassion must be so deep and His understanding of others so vast, that His heart can be linked by invisible lines of light to every human heart on the planet, as a towering figure of love, compassion, and power. His consciousness reaches to such lofty regions that He can transmit to this planet the Consciousness and the Power of the Second Person of the Trinity.

But in the work of the Hierarchy there are many departments, each requiring different qualifications, and each carrying on a different branch of the plan. Not only have the Seven Great Officials of the Rays Their major departments and Their group of associated administrators for the distribution of the force of each ray, but within the scope of each department are many sub-departments and many offices which require specialization.

There are many Masters, but there is only one Christ; and the qualifications for His Office are not the qualifications for all offices. One may find a parallel in the work of a great nation, for after all, the administration of a kingdom is based considerably upon the method of administering the planet, another evidence of the old saying, "As above, so below."

The king is the ruler of his people and the head of the government. The priests should meet the problems of man's emotional nature, giving him comfort and succor in his hour of tribulation. But there must be other departments dedicated to the service of the state and contributing directly to man's ultimate welfare and to the welfare of the kingdom which rarely contact the individual man at all.

Such a department is formed by the great scientists who are making researches which may ultimately benefit millions, but who could not possibly do their work except in isolation and free from interruptions. They may have very little personal sympathy with or understanding of the problems of an individual man, although devoting their lives to the welfare of humanity.

The Masters are not all Christs or Christs-to-be. They are filling posts in the complex government of the planet, posts won for Them by two great qualifications, equally necessary: the development of superior ability along special lines which made Them fitted to carry on Their special work, be it research or art or administration; and the willingness to carry on that work for the welfare of the world.

Sometimes one considers a Master merely a supremely good man. One forgets that to be a Master one must have mastered some function of human consciousness, and before one may be assigned to a post of any responsibility in any world one must have earned the right to the appointment by proven capacity. Virtue unaccompanied by knowledge and ability is of small service to humanity.

No man may attempt a degree of Master of Arts in any human university by good character alone; it must be accompanied by intellectual achievement; nor, on the other hand, can he attempt that degree, if virtue is not the accompaniment of intellect. The same law holds good in all worlds, and the Christ Himself has achieved His lofty position not only by the practice of compassion, but also by deep and prolonged study into the mystery of the human consciousness, so that He is an Adept in the understanding of the human heart, its motives, its trickeries, its treacheries, its sublime achievements, and its pitiful failures.

It is well to remember that during His appearance in Palestine, side by side with His compassion for the oppressed, rose His denunciation of the oppressors; there was not only His pity for the sinner, but His righteous wrath against the hypocrites, called by Him in unmistakeable language, "A generation of vipers".

Those Adepts Who are termed Masters, Those Who deal largely with masses of humanity, and Who are responsible for their evolution along executive or religious lines, are the only ones Who take pupils in the general sense of the word.

The other Adepts, Who might be called specialists, usually have about Them each a small group only, who are of Their own line and type, and who are fitted to share in Their peculiar work, and ultimately to become Their successors when They leave the planet. These Adepts one does not contact until one has achieved for oneself a high degree of proficiency in one of the special lines of research work, such as the manipulation of magical forces, profound knowledge of science, or of music.

If one met such Adepts, it is very doubtful if They would be recognized as Masters, for the dominant note would be science, or abstract thought rather than compassion or power, and many of the chelas of these Adepts are distinguished less by the pure compassion of the Christ and the overflowing love associated with it, than by dispassionate dedication of their services to the increase of knowledge for humanity.

CHAPTER X

The Tests of the Accepted Disciple

It is to be remembered that the first Initiation marks progress only to the point where the major part of a man's efforts in life will be dedicated to the service of mankind, and where also he will have achieved a certain measure of capacity, so as to guarantee that force put at his service will be used profitably.

In work for humanity, it is the disposition of all forces at the command of the pupil which counts. Whether it be money, whether it be health, whether it be strength, whether it be sympathy, whether it be spiritual resources that he has, all these must be disposed of to serve the greatest good of the greatest number, and to a very considerable degree, his work for any individual must be limited by the value of the services that individual can render to the work of the Lodge.

It is often hard to realize the need for cool and dispassionate thought in the conservation of energy, and in the wise disposal of one's time and resources. Initiates are primarily trustees, often with a given piece of work to do, to which the major part of their energies must be directed, and with only a small margin remaining for the casual requirements of friendship, associations and the general public.

Throughout the training of the chela he is tested for discretion, conservation, efficiency, and economy as well as dedication. His faults are judged more by how they interfere with his capacity for service than as factors in themselves. Almost all men have the weaknesses of their virtues, but these weaknesses are not judged by the conventional standards of the world.

Spite is far more seriously considered from the occult standpoint than the breach of conventional moral law, and the mind which rejoices in gossip less hopeful than one prone to anger. In the end, a man must meet all the weaknesses of his character and must achieve control in every vehicle and on every plane of nature, but the order in which those faults are corrected is not determined by the conventional emphasis of the world, and sins which come from lack of control range far lower and do far less harm than those allied to malice.

These latter sins are easily forgiven in the conventional world where gossip and slander are often reckoned as wit and where bigotry and intolerance pass for morality, but it is otherwise in the inner worlds. The measure of a man's morality is determined by the nature of his faults: whether they arise from a mean and cruel streak in his nature, or are merely the by-products of some great virtue not yet wholly governed.

The sweep of a wide and generous nature may often include failings which are unimportant hangovers from the past, and yet which may be harshly judged by the creeds of narrow natures. In occult work before all things bigness is necessary; generosity of heart and mind and spirit.

The measure of a man's service is determined not by his faults, but by what he accomplishes in spite of them, and narrow virtues which are often possessed by limited or still undeveloped natures may be swept aside and broken when the surge of a man's egoic power begins to pour through the channels of his mortal life.

Many a tranquil stream running quietly between well-defined banks becomes a rushing torrent which sweeps away ruthlessly anything which opposes it on its way to its objective, when the mountain snows add their volume of water to its own. So, many a controlled and balanced life breaks out in unexpected places under the downpouring of the new occult forces from the reservoirs of the Masters.

During the period when man is progressing from the point where he sets his foot upon the probationary Path until the time when he has achieved the occult rank of Arhat, his work is intensively the work of preparation. He is like a man who has entered the university, and who must graduate from it before he is really fitted to take up his greatest work in the world.

Such work as he does outside his curriculum must be a subsidiary outlet for his surplus energy, and a means of preventing his becoming too self-centered. But his major effort must be directed to self preparation, that he may more rapidly become available for trained service.

In the same way, the work of the chela is primarily one of preparation. For the sake of the work he has to do, he must achieve as rapidly as possible. Sometimes, therefore, those who are making a great effort on the occult path may seem to be doing very little in the world. Judged from the standpoint of worldly achievement they may have little to show.

None the less, those who can see into their inner consciousness know that they are being subjected to tests of ever increasing difficulty; that the vehicles are being strained to the utmost, and that in some cases they are, as it were, upon the rack, tortured to the limit of their capacity, to develop the sensitiveness of mind and body needful for the work, and at the same time to share, even though vicariously, the sorrows of human evolution, in order to understand the human heart, and thereby learn how to direct, guide, and comfort humanity.

Increasing pressure from the inner plane forces strains the nerves intolerably, yet steadfastness and endurance must be learned. Every desire of the personal life, little by little, must be burnt away, as dross is cleansed from gold, and in most cases this is done by pain, as the most rapid means for freeing the pure gold of the spirit from the dross of human weakness and desire. Renunciation after renunciation must be faced.

Often, none of this is apparent to the outer world, but within the consciousness of the chela the great fight is on, and the battleground, Kurukshetra, is his abiding place, until every weakness has fallen before the increasing power of his will and his sacrifice.

Not only this; not only must he conquer his own shortcomings; not only must he control the elemental forces which play through his nature and which are the heritage of evolution, those warring forces which built strength in the personality that the spirit might have a powerful instrument when at last it conquered the unruly will of its lower nature; but he must learn to find the Light within his own soul.

He must cease to lean upon the Master or upon God; he must become God, and feel the rise of divine power, of divine compassion and divine knowledge within his own heart. He must learn to stand uncomforted by any human love; he must learn to expect nothing from friendship and to give all. He must learn to accept injustice from the world without resentment, without surprise.

It is the law of the spiritual life that the man who wrests the treasures of occult knowledge and of occult power long guarded by the elementals for the service of man, must pay the price. He must meet the anger of those elementals, denuded of their sacred treasure, and he must meet the wrath of men, glamoured by these elementals to wreak their vengeance.

Hints of this strange law have come down to us through the ages in various mythologies; in the story of Sigurd and the Treasure of the Dragon; in the Tale of Prometheus.

These tests do not all come during the period of discipleship, but they are foreshadowed in the tests which the accepted disciple must meet, to be repeated in ever higher spirals as man progresses up the winding path to his goal.

It is because of the terrific severity of these inner tests given to those pressing forward to Initiation and beyond, that the plea goes forth to all who glimpse something of the occult law:

"Pour not the dross of criticism
Into the melting pot of discipleship."

All who tread the occult path are being tried beyond their strength, and they have need of the compassion and understanding of all students.

It is because the occult path brings much suffering; it is because the heart must be broken ere the personality relinquishes its will to the guidance of the ego; it is because those who have trod the Path even in small measure can scarcely endure the thought that others must suffer as they have suffered; it is because the Masters have anguished and bled and suffered; it is because They know the intolerable pain of evolution, that Their compassion is ever about the chela.

And when the darkness is greatest, when he seems to be utterly deserted alike by friend and Master; when he seems in a wilderness sombre and unillumined, utterly alone and hopeless even of God, then is the compassion of the Master most surely about him. For the Master understands in full the darkness and the despair that accompany some of the steps on the upward Path.

If those who have trod the Path only in part, and who

know something of the pain which is to come, have such
compassion for those who must follow in their footsteps
that they dread to have others face that which they themselves have undergone, in how much greater measure must
the compassion of the Masters be stirred.

It is said that the Lord Buddha, when He finally achieved
and looked back upon the dark and stormy path which He
had trod, had almost "deemed it all too hard for mortal feet,"
until the Spirit of the Earth seemed to cry out, "Surely I am
lost, I and my creatures; O Supreme! Let Thy Law be
uttered!"

The gateway of birth is fraught with agony, yet the physician must not stop the pangs, but must give courage to endure
and to achieve; so only can the race persist. The gateway to
the Kingdom of Heaven likewise is fraught with anguish, yet
can not the Great Physicians withhold the pain; only can
They give courage to enter and to achieve. So only can the
race achieve its heritage; so only can man pass from the bondage of the flesh to the liberation of the spirit.

Therefore, despite Their compassion, perhaps it is because
of Their compassion, that the race more speedily may pass
along the appointed way, sooner to escape the suffering which
the bondage of flesh exacts, Those who guide humanity stand
by and let the tests be given.

Despite the anguished cry of the tortured heart, They permit the disciple to suffer; They leave him in darkness, alone
and sometimes afraid, to find the Light; They give him
more than his strength can meet, for so is new strength gained;
They give him more than his heart can bear, for through the
portals of the broken heart flows the power of the spirit.

All this, and more. They do: for They would hasten and
not delay the birth pangs of the spirit. Great Physicians of the

soul, They seek to solace the world by urging men onward
through the Gateway of the Kingdom, for They know as
none but the Wise Ones of the earth can know, that the only
hope of lessening the anguish of humanity is through the
Path which leads to life eternal.

PART IV
Preparation for Initiation

CHAPTER XI
Relation to the Master

The time comes when such progress has been made that a candidate must start to prepare himself very definitely for Initiation. During all the period of accepted discipleship, the chela has been in close touch with some one of the Masters. This Master has undertaken to prepare him for Initiation. Before he was accepted as a disciple he had fulfilled the preliminary requirements of the Master Who took him on.

Every Master or teacher emphasizes the requirements a little differently. To some, certain qualities are paramount, and unless the candidate has them already to a marked degree, They will not even undertake his training. It is also probable that certain virtues are more important to one ray than to another. It may be this which determines the requirements of the various Masters.

When a Master undertakes to train a candidate He takes upon Himself a very great burden. All those who apply for such training should bear this strongly in mind. The Master is a man in a human body with many of the limitations of a human body.

When He takes a new body, which He has to do repeatedly, He takes a body which is a child of the race, with all the limitations and weaknesses which national consciousness, heredity and environment produce. He must take this very ordinary human body and train it and discipline it through many, many years, until it is in some measure capable not only of carrying through the high voltage forces which He needs in His work, but of reproducing, when necessary, upon a sensitized brain, those plans for the future which are in the archetypal world, enough of which He must bring down to guide Him in practical work on the physical plane. These are more or less like an architect's drawings, a guide for the constructive work He is to do, and His ability to do that work well depends first, upon the cognition of the plan; second, upon the training of His vehicles for use, so that He may influence directly or indirectly the humans and the nations with whom He is to work.

It is very doubtful whether any Master can do much with a new body until He has trained it for forty or fifty years. This, of course, is from the occult standpoint. If He is one of those upon the active rays, who constantly reincarnate in the arena of active life, He may train and key up the vehicles only to the point where He can accomplish the particular job He has in hand.

In other words, He may not make the effort necessary really to discipline and perfect the instrument, so that it may be a suitable vehicle for His higher powers. He may not undertake to eliminate all of the human faults which are woven into the fabric in which He has clothed Himself, and which belong to the race and to heredity; He may only discipline it sufficiently to meet the immediate need, and then drop it again promptly as soon as the particular work in hand is over.

This is perhaps a hard concept, but it is a very important one to grasp, lest we misjudge the Servers of mankind because we see some of the limitations of the rather crude instruments They have to use. But in any case, it is to be remembered that probably most of the Masters, except perhaps Those who live far away from human contact, have considerable limitations in the personality.

They are marked by two supreme qualities, *wisdom* and *absolute dedication* to the service of humanity, which result in the constant subordination of Their personal interests and desires, to the welfare of the work They are seeking to do.

They are bound by time and space. The resources and knowledge at Their command are distinctly limited. The strain to which They can submit Their physical bodies has a definite measure, and Their work as individuals is of necessity always secondary to the obligations of Their offices, for all of Them hold offices of greater or lesser responsibility, in regard to the supervision and directing of the planet upon the inner planes.

Some of the Masters are closely allied to political work, studying day and night the wisest methods to influence the leaders of the world into constructive paths. Others are closely allied to the deva work, and counsel with the Shining Hosts in the distribution of the forces to the planet which are at the command of the devas.

Other Masters are deeply engaged in research work which has to do with other members of the solar system, in studying how the planetary influences or extra solar system influences may be drawn to our aid and applied to problems here. Others again are concerned with the reception of visitors from other worlds, and the museums of records in which must be kept accurate replicas of all the important inventions of every age, and the various political changes which influence the well-being of the planet.

Still others are studying how to bring about physical and geographical conditions which shall make possible, in future ages, the unfoldment of those qualities required in new races;

for the constitution of the blood largely determines the powers latent in any human vehicle, and this constitution is changed by food, by air, by heat or cold, by noise or silence, by the very elemental essence which the mountains and lands and oceans breathe forth, by the minerals and magnetic areas which are built into the land long before it rises from the sea, by the composition of the soil and the resultant fauna and flora which there exist.

These are, in brief, some of the activities of the Masters. It is understandable, therefore, why so few Adepts feel Themselves at liberty to take personal pupils. Those Who do take personal pupils, in most cases, hold some definite official position for which They must prepare Their successors: and the pupils that They take are chosen with a view that, from among them, the most competent may be made the successor.

Again I repeat, a Master Who takes a new pupil takes upon Himself a very greatly added burden of responsibility and effort, and thereby definitely limits to some extent any other work that He wishes to do.

For once He has taken a pupil, until He definitely abandons him, He gives him much the same attention, solicitude, supervision and care that a mother does her only infant child, however little this may appear on the physical plane. It is a matter of constant concern to Him, and usually, constant disappointment, how the candidate responds.

It is almost impossible for a Master to draw anyone into close contact with Himself with whom He has not had strong personal ties through many lives. These strong personal ties of love, devotion and service, have built into the candidate certain capacities to respond harmoniously to the Master's vibration, which are a prerequisite to any training.

What the Master seeks to do for the pupil is to share with

him such knowledge, wisdom, power and understanding as the Master may have, and this may only be accomplished through that merging of consciousness and breaking down of the barriers of the mental body through deep and devoted affection on both sides.

Yet, however much He may love His pupil, and however close the tie may be, if the progress is not commensurate with the efforts expended, the Master will not be permitted to continue the relationship. He, too, has obligations which are paramount and to which the training of pupils must be secondary.

One can well understand, therefore, why those who desire to become candidates for Initiation are urged to give the utmost devotion and affection to the Master Whom they seek to serve, that by their love they may prepare to open themselves to His influence and to break down that shell which surrounds the mental body, so that as far as the Master is concerned, they may learn to blend their consciousness with His.

How true, indeed, is the old saying, that "The mind is the slayer of the Real", for it is that shell of egotism and self-centredness formed about the embryonic soul when it was seeking to hold for itself one individual human body, and which was its salvation at that time, which now becomes its greatest barrier and menace when it seeks to expand out of the limited self into the union of the spiritual life.

Before a candidate approaches a Master and asks for training, he should realize the sacrifice that he is requiring, and be prepared in turn to throw every power that he has of willing devotion and of aspiration into the task of fitting himself to make use to the fullest extent of the sacrifice that he is requiring.

CHAPTER XII

Requirements of Rays

Three Lords of the Law exist in space; the first is Master of the Elemental Forces in their original state; He hews the rock. The second is Master of Love, the light which purifies—of the fire which burns away the dross. He extracts the ore. The third is the Forger of Tools, and He is the Master of the Five Rays. He directs and guides and gives to each man that form of activity which shall be his.

The seven rays represent the seven major types of force in our system.

The requirements exacted of pupils of the different rays vary somewhat, dependent probably upon the type of force handled by each ray and its effects upon the vehicles. Certainly the 1st Ray is especially exacting in its requirements, perhaps because more responsibility devolves upon it for the guidance and control of other lives.

It should be borne in mind that although all rays work upon the physical plane, certain ones focus primarily there. These are the 1st, the 4th and the 7th. The 2nd and the 6th are especially focussed in the desire world, and the 3rd and 5th in the mental. Those rays which have to do with the conquest of physical matter in its densest form, are necessarily very exacting in the discipline they require as regards physical action.

It is the purpose of evolution on these rays as far as possible to achieve perfection of action, perfection of constructive knowledge in form building on the physical plane, and to that end pupils on these rays bring all resources of mind and heart to improve their technique in action.

The teachers of the 1st Ray lay especial emphasis upon truthfulness, honor, business integrity, courage, impersonality. Without these qualities already strongly entrenched in the nature, a candidate is rarely considered, let alone accepted.

Those who seek to achieve Initiation upon the 1st Ray will be called upon to lead others. They have the responsibility not only for their own lives, but for those of many others who will follow them. It is they who will be called upon to see the Vision for building the Race by which the people must be led. It is they who will be called upon to interpret the laws suitable to each new age. It is they who stand at the threshold of the world and draw from outer space those forces needed for the progress of the race, and it is they who direct those forces upon the race for its stimulation and development.

How absolute is the necessity, therefore, that they see clear. How absolutely necessary that they do not compromise with truth, that no latent fear or dishonesty or personal desire sway them from that undeviating line of rectitude which alone can mark the way safely for their people. It devolves upon them to lay the foundation stones upon which the whole future structure of civilization is to be built, and that foundation must be strong and accurate and sound, since upon it all the future must rest.

Power is achieved through rigid discipline of the vehicles

so that they become at once accurate and flexible, responsive to whatever task is put to them, and yet so cleansed of elemental desire, that the pupil remains utterly impersonal. This needs a very nice tempering of the three vehicles, and every latent weakness must be hammered out.

Not that an absolutely God-like human is to be created: probably as long as we live in an imperfect world where we must use the crude products of our present humanity, as long as we are bombarded by the tempests of evil and destructive thought forms which at present sweep our planet, the strain which the occultist puts upon his vehicles will result in certain human faults and failings even among the greatest.

But faults and failings will come not from fundamental weaknesses of the nature, but will be due merely to the passing stress and strain to which the vehicles are subjected. Foibles of personal taste, nerve strain when sensitive vehicles are exposed to the noise of our civilization. impatience temporarily, when blocked by the stupidity of the human material which must be moulded, heartsickness at the coarseness and crudity which still exist in our world, heartbreak at the cruelty and suffering which lie like an evil cloud over the progress of humanity—these may appear.

Under the constant assault of such problems which the occultist can never forget, as may the average human immersed in personal pleasures, the vehicles react at times to strain like any human body, but the purpose to serve and the will to serve and the power to serve never falter.

The requirements of the 2nd and 6th Rays differ from the 1st. Here devotion, compassion and tenderness must appear in a very high degree. These two rays have to do more with the training of the individual than with the development of races. As in the past it has been recognized that the functions of state and church differed widely in their responsibilities, so do the duties of the rays differ.

The 1st, the 4th and the 7th Rays deal with humanity as a whole, with government, with organization, and they must follow the law of their kind, that the welfare of the whole must take precedence to the welfare of the individual.

In the outer world, in many religions, in order that the individual hardships which result from the law of organization and government may be mitigated, the church offers the confessional and the solace and comfort of the priests to the individual, promising that the confessions of the individual which are necessary for the relief of the anguished soul shall not come under the jurisdiction of the law which would be obliged to exact punishment.

Law must exist for the welfare of the whole, but mercy and solace must be given to sinners when they repent of their sins, to prevent the disintegration of the human soul. In all great civilizations these distinctions have been recognized, and the duty of the priest and of the ruler have, therefore, differed, so that all human needs might be met by one group or the other.

Hence, it is clear why the requirements of the 2nd and 6th Rays will be differently emphasized from the active rays. In time he who will become a Master must gain a considerable degree of all virtues, but in the beginning the emphasis will be differently placed. Tenderness, compassion, forgiveness, knowledge is required on the 2nd Ray. For this ray must be not only the comforter but the teacher; not only the priest but the physician, and charity is more important than some more executive qualities.

The 3rd and 5th Rays which are focussed principally upon the mental plane, have in turn other requirements. They represent the intelligence aspect, in many ways more akin to the 1st in their requirements than to the 2nd. They represent science with its great impersonality; the conquest of the forces of nature, with the high requirements of courage, precision and accuracy, perfection of detail, great impersonality of mind.

They concern themselves less with the welfare of humans as individuals than either of the other two groups. The 1st Ray must train its leaders and study the comfort and happiness of the race. The 2nd must work for the welfare of each individual soul. The 3rd and 5th Rays deal with great organizations in which achievement requires the subordination of the individual to gain the highest fruits of co-operation. Theirs is the standard of the hive, where the welfare of the hive rises supreme and all individual needs are dwarfed thereby.

They it is who will ultimately have the governing of this planet, when the world shall have been organized so that all people have their appointed place in the great organization which they can fill wisely and well. We see the forerunners of these future rulers of the world, and the organization of the world, in the great businesses which now exist, and which foreshadow that complete world organization of the future.

Then all rays existing on the planet will be subordinated to the great Third aspect of life. The 1st Ray will have served its purpose and passed on, leaving behind its organizers in the 4th and 7th. There will be no further need for priests and seers, for all men will be serving the planet to the glory of God, and the 2nd Ray too will pass onward.

The reflection of the 2nd Ray will appear in the teachers and in the functions of the personal relations courts, and similar agencies in the big corporations; and there will remain in activity but the five rays from the 3rd to the 7th which are in reality the only ones which belong to the three lower planes of manifestation upon which humans normally function.

CHAPTER XIII

Qualifications for Initiation

When the time approaches for the Master to present the chela for Initiation, the chela must prove to the satisfaction of the Brotherhood that he is fit for power to be bestowed upon him. He must pass certain definite tests to prove the progress he has made, and before taking these tests he must weed out the faults of the personality which would prevent him from being a selfless and efficient instrument.

The qualifications are divided into four major parts. One description of them is:

      I: Point of view,
     II: Renunciation,
    III: Power,
    IV: Sacrifice.

These points have been variously stated, and are sometimes called Discrimination, Desirelessness, Good Conduct, and Love. Perhaps they may be analyzed from another point of view in such a way as to throw added light upon the practical problem of attainment.

The ground which has been covered earlier has brought the chela through the preliminary tests. He has turned from the world and set his foot upon the swift upward path. He has met the tests of the elementals, and has not been turned from his chosen way. He has proven his devotion to the

Master and his desire for service. He must now with the knowledge he has gained train and discipline his personality.

He must prove not only his desire, but his capacity to succeed, and through all the hours of waking consciousness in every action of the day he must see the opportunity to discipline his vehicles and prove his powers. The following pages seek to show in the most practical way the application of the laws of discipleship to daily life.

I. Point of View or Orientation

It has been said that the greatest gift a Master can give to His pupil is a change in his point of view. As one passes through the seven ages of man from childhood to maturity, the most noticeable change is that in the point of view.

The high lights of childish joy fade as the desires of adolescence arise. The desires of adolescence make way for the ambition and the mental achievement of maturity. The difference between the moron and the average man, and between the average man and the leader, and between the leader and the Master, lies largely in the difference in what each considers important in life.

It is an increasing discrimination between relative values, between the important and the unimportant, which marks maturity of soul. The Master seeks to teach the chela the point of view of the Son of God, that in the light of divine wisdom he may see life as it truly is, and choose rightly between the essential and the non-essential.

Only as man understands the purpose of life and the path he must tread to divinity, only as his consciousness soars beyond the limitations of the planet and all planetary life, only as he glimpses something of the whole Plan in its vast majesty, can he discriminate wisely as to actions in daily life.

The history of humanity shows that growth and civilization are marked by a gradual changing of values; those things admired by the savage and primitive man—brute force and ruthless courage—are not the virtues which are most valuable, and, therefore, most valued in the civilized man.

Not only has his environment changed, so that powers of mind are more essential than powers of body, but the old virtues have lost their significance and have been supplanted by more complex and intellectual concepts. Honor, truthfulness, unselfishness, sacrifice, have become the virtues which have built a useful system where man curtails his own liberties for the sake of peace and good will in the group.

In like manner, those virtues which belong to the man of the world must be supplanted by new virtues in the occultist. Just as the virtues of the brute, necessary to his environment, are out of place in the civilized man, so the virtues of the civilized man, however necessary and valuable to him in the outer world, must often be radically modified in the occult life.

The devotion to family and friends which is the keystone of our civilization, must become secondary to those virtues of the occultist, loyalty to the work and to the service of humanity. Yet just as the brute force which has taught the primitive man to defend his own home, lays the foundations for that loyalty and sacrifice for the family which marks the best type of civilized man, so the virtues of the civilized man lead directly to the more impersonal virtues of the occultist.

In no way are the standards of the occultist relaxed. On

the contrary they are more stringent; but, as in the army a soldier's first loyalty is to his duty rather than to his family, even at the sacrifice of the best welfare of his family, so the loyalty of the occultist to his work and to the welfare of humanity transcends the love and devotion which he feels for his own.

Indeed, this must be so, for as he progresses in power and begins to direct and disburse the occult resources of the planet, he must be above the temptation of seeking to use them for the aggrandizement of his own, just as the disburser of public funds must be above the temptation of diverting any of these for the use of his own family.

The Brotherhood is indeed a pledged army; pledged to guard and protect the planet as far as lies in Its power, from evil and destructive forces; and pledged as soldiers are pledged, to put the welfare of the whole above the welfare of any individual, however dear to them.

One can see from this how our human institutions, such as the army of defense, are preparing the way for those final great responsibilities which lie upon the shoulders of the Brotherhood and of the Hierarchy. With all its horrors, war in the past has nevertheless harnessed the destructive energies of man in such a way as to do the least damage so that he gradually learned the virtues of obedience, self sacrifice, loyalty and idealism.

For every soldier is taught, and profoundly believes, that he is fighting for the salvation of his people against the encroachments of a dangerous enemy. Only through struggle and conflict in the past have the nations gained the discipline which they needed.

The time has now come, however, in the evolution of the

planet where the great wars of empire can no longer serve
the best good of the world, and the virtues won in that
terrible school must be developed by less savage and brutal
means, and perhaps modified and supplanted by other virtues
which will be developed through co-operation and peace.

In daily life we often see men risk their lives, and thereby
the safety and well-being of their families, in some desperate
venture for the service of others; the fireman in his field, the
soldier, the coast guards, especially the doctors and nurses
who go to nurse the plague striken or the wounded. Is it,
therefore, not suitable that he who aspires to enter the
Guardian Band of the planet, with its vast responsibilities and
great powers, should be prepared to pledge a loyalty to that
service which shall take precedence to the needs of his own
family in times of *emergency*, just as these other servers of
humanity have done?

Perhaps some of those who have heard of Initiation and
of the Masters and of the occult path, look upon it more as
a matter of personal progress, of personal illumination and
increased vision. Some of these things may come, but what
a candidate really does is to offer his services to the most
difficult, the most dangerous, the most exacting and the
most self-sacrificing task which falls to the lot of mankind.

Entering the Brotherhood entails superhuman strain, un-
ending responsibility, constant attack from destructive forces,
and the constant necessity for ever-increasing discipline and
selflessness of the personality. Yet, throughout the ages, men
have leaped forward to sacrifice and service, moved by the
glory of ideals, disregarding comfort and pleasure, love and
companionship, in a desperate cause; and so, today, in spite
of all the exactions, men and women are seeking to enter

the Brotherhood to share Its responsibilities, Its pains and Its sacrifices.

Yet, those who offer themselves as candidates would do well to remember that the exactions are heavy; that they must be ever on guard; that they must never for a moment relax their efforts to move forward to the loftier heights before them. For upon this precipitous Path one may not stand still. If one does not go forward, one slips backward, and unless one's mind is kept constantly oriented to the vision of the goal, one cannot see the Path clearly amid the dusty highways of the world.

It is the point of view of the Master—of the paramount importance of the work, of the necessity for the service to the race, and of duty before which all other duties are dwarfed—which is the first requisite of the candidate for the Path of Initiation.

Be it clear that service to the world does not relieve one of personal responsibilities. When the soldier is not called upon to fight he must fulfill the duties of his family life, the duties of the citizen, the duties of the son, father and husband. Similarly, the occultist unless a greater duty arises clear and unmistakable, must fulfill his family obligations to the uttermost. Indeed, his family obligations within reason, provided he does not permit any member of his family to enslave him or to determine for him what are his obligations, form part of his service to humanity.

As he protects, educates and cares for those dependent upon him, he performs a certain necessary part in the social scheme, and therefore, a part in the planetary scheme. But he must bear always in mind his occult responsibilities, that he may see his worldly duties in the proper perspective. It is this necessary discrimination between the essential and the non-essential, between the greater and the lesser duty, which gradually marks the growth of wisdom in the Initiate and probationer.

The goal of humanity is the development of judgment, for judgment is the flower of the creative mind. Love is the matrix within which judgment must grow, but judgment is the quality, through the unfoldment of mind, which humanity must gain. The growth of wisdom marks the progress of the soul through all the cosmic schemes, and wisdom can come only through wise judgment based upon discrimination.

II.   Renunciation or Desirelessness

The next great qualification is usually expressed as renunciation or desirelessness. It is the gradual tearing loose of those tentacles which hold us to the personal life, of the multitude of small personal desires which govern and make up for the most part our personality. One must lose the fear of life, and the fear of death, and the fear of loss of comfort. And yet, these virtues every soldier practices perforce. They are harder to achieve without that fine fire of enthusiasm which lights the soldier in his duty, with the mass emotion of a great emergency.

The human tree has its roots in the ground, and it clings to the earth and feels that all the majesty of its leafy head comes from its strong grip upon the soil. And this is true. The power and success of the personal life depend a good deal upon its grip on the physical plane, and upon the multitude of little desires that run out like tentacles and hook on to various aspects of physical being.

Tear these ruthlessly asunder, and the very life force of the incarnation dies. It dies down into indifference, into lethargy and into death. This is what does happen at death, and why so often indifference precedes death, particularly after a long illness.

Such destruction must be avoided. Those tentacles which lead to strength and power must not be torn loose until they can be re-established above in the impersonal worlds to feed the impersonal life. Instead of drawing their sustenance from the earth, they must draw their sustenance from the spiritual worlds. Instead of reaching upward to take, the individuality must lean downward to give, and rooted in that world of divine power and love must find strength above to pour down to those still rooted in the lower worlds below.

Personal desires must be consumed by the flame of devotion. The personal life must be distilled, so that it becomes spiritual essence, remembering always that without that personal life there could be no spiritual essence. As the orchid draws its sustenance from the air and seeks no contact with the rich soil of earth, so the occultist must draw his life from the inner worlds, seeking no comfort, no sustenance, no support from the life of the personality.

We see a symbol of the occult life in the great Tree Yggdrasill of Norse Mythology whose roots were deep in the heavens and whose trunk and branches touched the earth.

Desirelessness, in the truest sense, means selflessness. Only as the selfishness and self-centredness of the human heart is cleansed away in the Light of Spiritual Vision can the personal self render that obedience to the will of the divine universal Soul whereby alone it can achieve divinity.

It is necessary to carry this desirelessness to a very high degree of perfection. For as one clings to form, as one clings to the habits of the body, and the comfort of the body, one fails often to leap forward to seize what may prove a supreme opportunity. The shot and shell of the battlefields, the danger and discomfort of wounds, do not daunt the ardent soldier from volunteering for desperate service.

But it is easy in the personal life to be turned aside from an opening door to the higher life, by some small complex of the lower mind, which, with its small grasping desires, its preferences and dislikes, clouds the intuitive vision of the true path.

Desirelessness does not require asceticism. One should not renounce the joy in beauty, nor the capacity for love and tenderness, nor the power of affection for those near and dear to us. Renunciation requires freedom from the grip of the elementals so that a man may use or refrain from using any force in the body, as he thinks best. It is not necessary to refrain from food. It is necessary only to control the appetite, that wisdom and not desire guide it.

This is true of all physical functions. The Master is a Master because He is master of Himself: not because He acts or refrains from acting in any particular way, but because He is free through conquest of Himself from the blinding of wisdom by desire. There is no function in the physical body which has not its Godlike purpose. But undeveloped man is the pawn of Nature, which guides his actions by magic spell and glamour into the channels She desires for the fulfillment of Her purposes.

Until a man is released from glamour, until he is no longer guided by passion, by wrath, by greed, by lust, he is not free. Once free, he may use or not use, any of his powers, mental, emotional and physical, as wisdom directs, and not be bound thereby.

There is no virtue in asceticism by itself, except insofar as it is a means to an end, to teach man self-conquest. But the purpose of life is not asceticism. It is self-mastery. Therefore, the Master marries or not as best serves the purpose of the divine plan. We know that the Manus must marry, not occasionally, but repeatedly through many lives, that They may build the type. Marriage in itself is not incompatible with the occult path, but never must the occultist permit himself to be dominated by any elemental force, for therein lies danger.

Renunciation means the complete subjugation of the personal will to the divine will. It means the attainment of true selflessness in the service of man and God.

CHAPTER XIV
Qualifications (Continued)

III. Power

The third qualification—Power—requires the development of all the force latent in the vehicles, roused, purified and directed by the divine flame of spiritual will. Only awakened spiritual fire can carry a man onward through the trials, ordeals and dangers of the Path. Indeed the spiritual will is that alone which can at last permit the lower personality to achieve divinity and conscious continuity. The Kingdom of Heaven is taken by storm, and only by the stormy power of atma, reflected in the lower vehicles, can the great assault be accomplished. It is hard to speak with emphasis enough of the need for this awakening. Indeed without it all else is valueless. For without it the spiritual worlds are forever sealed.

Through the power of will intensive and penetrating as the blue-green flame of an acetylene torch the vehicles may be purified, aligned, trained, and perfected so as to become a powerful and skillful instrument for the Divine Self.

Once a man has gained somewhat of the true point of view, once he has freed himself from the tentacles of desire, he is ready to begin the attainment of power.

It must be a beautifully trained and perfected instrument in the three worlds, that he offers to the Master.

Power depends upon skill in action directed by a flaming will. The man must begin to polish and perfect all the powers of the personality. Many people in aspiring to the spiritual life, tend to neglect the personality, to disregard it, to seek to dwell in a realm of fancy far removed from the grossness of the physical plane.

This is diametrically opposed to the plan and purpose of evolution. We are here in the three worlds of form to perfect an instrument whereby the worlds of form, and the powers therein, may be mastered. The personality, which includes the mind, emotions and body, corresponds to the Third Person of the Trinity, the Holy Ghost.

The Holy Ghost is the principle behind all manifestation of form, whether it be cosmos, system, planet or individual, plant, molecule or atom. We dwell today in the kingdom of the Holy Ghost and we dwell therein by virtue of a set of vehicles called the personality which have been created by the help of the Holy Ghost for the purpose of gaining conquest over the forces latent in manifested form.

The essence of the personalities never dies, and though the time may come when the Holy Ghost and the Son are both drawn up into the Father during the Night of Brahma; yet when manifestation recurs, as recur it must, the Holy Ghost will again manifest in form, and any individual whether it be human, superhuman or divine, which desires to function in the worlds of manifestation must use those forms which represent the Holy Ghost in himself, and which he has built up with care and endless effort in the realms of personality by repeated incarnations in form.

We are wont, many of us, who aspire to the vision of the higher worlds, to discount and belittle the place and purpose of the personality. When esoteric students talk of their egos

and their monads as being of consequence, it is well to remember that these are occupied in their own spheres; that
they exist as entities only for the purpose of contacting those
spheres in which they function, and are but remotely concerned with the problems of the personality.

The personality must attain for itself, must win for itself
the conquest of its own kingdom, the worlds of form. It is
only as it succeeds here on this physical earth in meeting successfully the requirements and exactions of physical life, that
it can ultimately obtain liberation from this planet.

The purpose of incarnation in form is to develop the
powers latent in form, to unfold, control and direct them.
When the personality has thus mastered its own kingdom,
it is ready to co-operate with its divine Master. It has fulfilled the end of the plan of incarnation and can become an
effective instrument in the hands of its Higher Self for successful work in future worlds of form.

Ultimately, the worlds of form are dissolved and the
essence drawn into the Universal Life, but surely not until
they have reached the highest point of perfection possible in
the present manifestation. We, in turn, cannot expect to be
freed from the limitations of this planet until we have made
of our personality so skillful and perfect an instrument that
it has mastered the forces of the three lower worlds.

"Circumstances?" said Napoleon, "I make circumstances!"
So must the personality conquer the limitations of the
worlds in which it dwells. Then, and then only, is it prepared to ask for release. A release from incarnation in the
worlds of form can be but temporary, since sooner or later a
spirit will wish to use once more the powers gained in the
worlds below. And then that vehicle which it will build
for that new world of form on some far distant planet or

system, can be made up only of those powers which it has gained here during its successive personalities on this planet.

Therefore, the way of power is the way of conquest, and the way of conquest is the way of discipline: the conquest, co-ordination and training of the three vehicles of the personality.

Under the heading of Power are six sub-headings: enthusiasm, faith, courage, skill in action, impersonality, and obedience. All these are necessary to the unfoldment of the power latent in the vehicles.

It must be remembered that the purpose of the occultist differs from the purpose of the average good man of the world. With the occultist, the achievement of virtue is but the preliminary step to the achievement of power. Virtue must safeguard the use of power, but virtue without power can accomplish little. In the higher worlds no man without virtue can be considered. but no man without power can be accepted.

Enthusiasm. First upon the list comes enthusiasm, perhaps one of the most gracious and divine qualities in nature, and without which no soul can travel through the rocky fastnesses and shadowed crevasses of the Path of Initiation. It is the motive power of all endeavor, the mainspring of all effort and without it there is no progress.

Where enthusiasm fails, life fails, and in achieving desirelessness one must be careful to guard the sacred flame of enthusiasm. It is that which replenishes courage, it is that which gives the power to rise again after repeated failure, it is that which makes it possible to take the Kingdom of Heaven by storm.

Without it the interminable training and discipline of the

nature would become intolerable. Without it joy would cease, and without joy, whether it be joy in service or joy in beauty, or joy in love, without joy, life becomes unendurable and physical forces ebb. When we lose the joy in physical plane delights, when the normal force of the elementals has been diverted, it is only the divine fire of enthusiasm which comes from the inner worlds that gives us the strength to carry on.

Faith. Closely related to enthusiasm is faith. Not a blind faith, not a narrow faith, not a dogmatic faith, but faith in the capacity of man to achieve divinity; faith in the ultimate beneficence of the Plan; faith in the wisdom and goodness of those inspired and loving Entities Who guard and govern our system and Who are for us, perhaps, best represented by the term God; by that all-embracing Tenderness and Love which watches over the destiny of earthly man.

As man sets his foot upon the rocky path of occultism, as he aspires to the divine heights of achievement, he must prove himself conqueror of the destructive forces of the planet, and step by step as he goes upward, he is exposed to the assaults of the various destructive forces of wrath and fear and hatred, of despair and darkness, of loneliness and doubt, in a way which no ordinary man can conceive, protected as he is by the Guardian Wall which the Masters and Adepts form about the schoolroom in which most humans function.

Just as the child in school cannot conceive the evil which exists in some of the more degraded spots of the earth because he is protected by his parents and teachers, so the average man rarely contacts those destructive elemental forces which assail the candidate, and of those forces perhaps the most terrible and destructive is doubt.

Not doubt in any particular phase, not doubt in any particular plan, not that reasonable questioning of any particular path. all of which is necessary to every step forward, but that devastating doubt closely allied to despair, which makes the world seem futile and dreams of divinity hopeless and unreal.

In the dark periods through which every soul must pass, where there seems no light anywhere, no help anywhere, no strength within himself, he must hold by faith, by faith and hope, until the darkness lightens. Lighten it will and must, if he truly have faith in the ultimate beneficence and wisdom of the Plan. A man may lose faith in any individual, he may lose faith in any leader and probably will. He may lose faith in any particular way or plan, but he must keep that ultimate faith that there is a Path, in order that when his footsteps falter and fail, when he loses the Path, he may through faith find courage to seek and find it once more.

Every man must face the darkness that little by little the light of his own soul may shine forth; but he will face it more successfully if he can hold always like a beacon light of the soul, that faith in the beneficence of God which in time will no longer remain a matter of faith, but shall become knowledge.

Courage. No man may tread the Path of Initiation without courage. that diamond quality which one sees shining so bright in the human race under adversity. One must have courage to attempt the Path. One must have courage to tread the Path. One must have courage to attain the citadel. Courage to venture where the mass of humanity will not follow. Courage to bear the jeers which attend the lonely seeker. Courage to do right at any cost. Courage to surmount those destructive forces which can be surmounted by courage alone. Courage to dare and courage to do.

Courage is not recklessness. Recklessness is often motivated by fear; fear to stop, and so to face the danger judiciously. It is haste to action without caution or judgment. True courage ultimately will lead the sons of man out of the pit of error and doom into which they have fallen.

Skill in Action. These three qualities assured, as the matrix within which he can unfold his powers, the candidate turns his will to the training of himself in skill in action which is after all the means of conquest of the lower worlds. Skill in action means efficiency in every active department of life; without it no man may progress far in any world.

Capacity and ability are even more valuable to the Occult Hierarchy than to the business world, and certainly more necessary, as greater issues are involved.

To gain capacity one must have, first, accuracy. Without the ability to receive instructions accurately and accurately to carry them out, no one may go far on any path. There must be accuracy of vision, accuracy of memory, of sight, and of observation. There must be accuracy of speech, and in fact all those accuracies which make a good business man, a good soldier, and a good occultist.

As one progresses in the occult world one enters into a vast laboratory full of dangerous elements and destructive forces. One is trained by the chief chemist or chief laboratory leader gradually to manipulate and handle these dangerous forces. The ability to carry out instructions accurately in the tiniest detail is more essential in the occult world, therefore, than in a high power machine shop or chemical laboratory. Far greater destruction may result in the inner worlds from the failure to carry out instructions accurately than on the physical plane, although on the physical plane it may result in the death of thousands.

Next, there must be promptness. No one who has not a sense of the value of time can go far on the occult path. He who is not prompt and who thus wastes the time of others, fails himself in an occult duty. The power to do a thing at a given time, to have necessary things ready at the appointed time, so to manipulate forces on the physical plane that engagements and agreements may be depended on, is of value equally to the business man and to the occultist.

Another occult qualification is business rectitude or integrity. Money, although a symbol, is a symbol of something holy. It is a symbol of human labor. It is also that accumulated reserve which makes possible the gradual lift of the race from savagery, the opening up of new countries and new resources, that in time well-being and comfort may be given to all members of this troubled planet.

Money should be respected. Not for its powers to bring luxury, but for its power to raise the race to those heights which shall free it from the brute labor of the past. There is a strange occult reaction to debt in any form, and the man who is solvent, and the organization that is solvent, and the nation that is solvent, face the world with a courage which only solvency can give.

One of the great occult lessons that all humans must learn is not to contract for that for which they cannot pay. Debt has a corroding and suffocating effect on spiritual life and spiritual forces. Therefore, business integrity which ranks so high in the business world, ranks perhaps even higher in the spiritual.

Wise administration of money comes in under this head, too, for it is one of the resources of the planet, and the would-be occultist must learn to administer wisely every resource at his command, whether it be health or time or money.

I have likened occultism to business because efficiency is the keynote of business, the keynote of the great races of the future: because our coming civilizations are to be built upon the virtues which business inculcates, upon the qualities of the great Third Aspect which business represents.

There have been three great types of civilization. One is empire built—built by the warriors; one, the priest rule—built upon the religions and teachings of the priests. Now comes the third, built upon the power of organization and the training which comes through co-operation and efficiency in business, and which is to shape the future races.

Tact. The final quality of efficiency is tact, that skill in action, skill in speech, which teaches us to work harmoniously with others, needed in all worlds. The occultist must ever be dealing with humans. He will destroy his efficiency by personal shortcomings of disposition or of understanding.

Under these various headings, come the requirements of skill in action, requirements which will prepare the candidate to be of some use in the physical world, and without which, however lofty his aspirations, however benevolent his intentions, he may lamentably fail.

Impersonality. Perhaps the most marked difference between the big man and the little man of the business world, is the power of the big man to accept and apply criticism. No one can go far on any path who is not eager to learn. To learn one must welcome criticism and apply it.

Impersonality alone can truly value criticism, and impersonality arises from that true humility of spirit which knows its own divinity and need not pander to personal vanity.

During the earlier stages of evolution, for his protection

in a world of strife, man surrounded himself with self-created glamour.   Otherwise he could not have endured his own crudities and deficiencies, but as man seeks to achieve he must learn to destroy this glamour, and to see himself truly, else he cannot round out his nature and attain that balance required of the Adept.

Every man has the vices of his virtues.   He has the limitations of his unique line of development, and he has gone his own way for so many incarnations that there are warps in his nature which he cannot recognize.   It is here that the teacher gives his greatest service, for he helps the pupil destroy the glamour which blinds him, and shows him incisively the weaknesses he must conquer.

But again only impersonality can gain full value from this service.   That pride which disguises itself as mortification, as inferiority complex, as discouragement, destroys the value of the Master's counsel.   Impersonality accepts criticism gladly and raises a man almost to the threshold of divinity. It is the quality which makes the unknown soldier, without which no great achievement can be won.

Obedience. Finally, as part of the achievement of power, comes the quality of obedience. No man who cannot obey can command.   And the Occult Hierarchy in the Inner Worlds is based upon the law of receiving commands from your superiors and giving commands to those below you.   Therefore, the power to give obedience is necessary.   Probably the greatest vice which man has to fight is that of disobedience.

One should not be obedient to all people.   One should not be at all times obedient to constituted authorities, else some of the great reforms and revolutions of the world could never have been achieved.   But one must give the most perfect and

complete obedience to those whom we recognize as our occult
teachers and leaders in all matters which relate to the training
we are being given, during the time of our training. Later
one obeys only the Higher Self.

One may at any time disagree in opinion or policy with
one's teacher, but in all matters of occult training one must
either obey one's teacher or abandon him, just as one must
obey one's chemical professor while experimenting in the
laboratory or leave the laboratory. It is a very delicate matter
of discrimination, and one is always at liberty to leave the
laboratory when one loses confidence in one's professor.

But it is neither fair nor safe to continue to experiment
in the professor's laboratory and disobey the instructions
which he gives. Most of all one must attain the abstract
power of obedience, which depends upon accuracy and precision, upon intelligence and judgment, so that one may grasp
accurately the instructions given and carry them out faith-
fully.

Those who have not been trained in obedience rarely have
the precision and accuracy which permits them to take instructions successfully, and those who cannot take instructions
successfully, cannot profit by instruction. In other words,
it is useless to teach those people who have not learned to
carry out instructions successfully, and this applies on all
planes.

Furthermore, obedience includes the willingness to give up
one's own will in all things which concern the greater good.
As a candidate progresses on the path, as he makes his links
with his teachers and begins to live the life of the Initiate, he
must learn to hear that inner voice which is scarcely more
than a shadow of feeling to protect him from error.

He must learn to check himself and listen before action and speech, however seemingly unimportant, to see whether he has the occult right to do what he plans. In time when he finds himself about to travel on the wrong path, he will gain a curious sense of discomfort which will warn him to reconsider his plans.

He must be prepared at any moment to abandon his own plans, no matter how carefully thought out, if he gets that slight check which warns him that they are not in line with the Great Plan, and the quality of obedience to his own inner self alone can win for the candidate that power to gain the inner response as to the correctness or wisdom of his actions, that perfect submission to the will of the greater SELF which permits the light of the divine mind at times to guide and illumine the lesser vehicle.

Lastly, through obedience only can he become the divine instrument. For as he brings himself under the training of discipline, so that his own vagrant desires and vagrant will are reined and checked, he at last is prepared to become the son of the Father, the obedient assistant of his Higher Self.

He never becomes the Higher Self until that far distant period when the personality must cease, but he becomes the willing co-operator in the worlds of form, the obedient servant to those rays of wisdom and guidance which fall from the chariot wheels of his Divine Self, to mark the path he must follow.

IV. Sacrifice

The final great quality is sometimes called love, and sometimes sacrifice—sacrifice, in the sense of making all things sacred. Love in its highest sense is sacrifice, for it sanctifies all things that it touches, but in some ways the word sacrifice, if it is understood to include love may be better understood. It means the sanctification of the life; the making of all things holy. It means the offering of every resource of mind, heart and body, of effort, of family and possessions to God and to the service of man.

Ere the occultist or the Initiate can become the Master or the Adept he must have won, have wrested from himself, the utmost treasures that the personality has to offer, and laid them before the Great White Throne. He must know that neither hatred nor malice nor vengeance can ever again tempt him from the service of the race.

He must *know* that no personal love, no personal tie can ever make him falter in allegiance to the highest that he visions; that he is free, not from love but from that elemental urge which sweeps humans on like a rushing wind, so that in the service of their beloved one they know neither good nor evil, they know only what they call love. From this he must be free, for at all times his vision must remain unclouded in his service to mankind.

This great elemental force has been the teacher of humanity, teaching it sacrifice and unselfishness. But it has the danger that it often so seizes possession of the man or woman that they are helpless before it, and driven by their consuming passion commit crimes against the public welfare for the sake of the one they love.

This can never be in the Master; however great His love, it must be guided always by the laws of right and justice, by the welfare of the race. The Adept must be content to ask nothing of life, He must be prepared to give. There will always be those, perhaps, whom He loves more tenderly than others, His own people who will follow Him through the Gateway and perhaps become the component parts of a group soul of which He is the central atom.

Of these things we know little. But the wisest teachers that we know had Their favorite disciples, not that They loved the others less, but that They loved the one more, because They were more akin in spirit, more near that union without barriers which we shall know when we are no longer bounded by the limitations of the personality.

But when at last every act, every thought, every word becomes sanctified by the spirit of love and unselfishness, by the desire to serve, by the will to follow the Light of God, then is man prepared either to carry on the work of God here, or to enter into other worlds to carry on His Will there. He will then have learned the lesson of the planet, he will then have conquered the desires of the personality and won his divinity by sanctifying his powers to the service of God.

The sum of all this discipline which leads to power, the most valuable result of all this training in desirelessness, in orientation, in discipline and in sacrifice, will be judgment. Perhaps the most comprehensive virtue that is wholly human may be summed up in the word judgment. Because good judgment alone can make effort, service and sacrifice valuable to mankind.

It was to attain the jewel of judgment, the divine gift of creative mind, that the Sons of God began their long pilgrimage through human incarnation, and when the pupil has seen the Star of Initiation, when he has proved his knowledge of good and evil by the development of good judgment, then, and then only, is he ready to serve the world.

CONCLUSION
The Great Law

Throughout man's long path of ascent ever before him gleams the goal of the narrow Gateway of Liberation. Through this he must pass to gain his heritage, and when he reaches at last the snowy peaks of consciousness which mark the Adept. he will have fulfilled the purpose of human incarnations.

From these heights he will determine whether he shall go on to other realms of experience and service or turn back to help his younger brethren to achieve as he has achieved. Only on the far side of the Gateway of Initiation can man know himself. Stripped of personal desire and personal pride he enters into the life of conscious union with The Great Law which determines the plan for all humanity.

Once he glimpses this Law, once he pledges himself to co-operate with It, he begins to gain knowledge and wisdom to help this darkened Star. Before that all is darkness and he cannot see how to serve, for the darkness in his own mind. Only as he learns to know not intellectually, but from true inner knowledge. the truth of the purpose of life and the method of achievement, can he truly help mankind. The greatest need in all of life is the change of heart which marks the change from selfishness to self-sacrifice and selflessness.

Through the narrow gate of self-sacrifice. where it is stripped of all possessions, must pass the soul on its journey to fulfillment and liberation. At the gate are attendant devils who whisper of the lost pleasures he forsakes who turns his face from the world, lost joys, lost comforts, lost securities, which are indeed only phantoms, but which lure the mind of the unperceiving. When a man at last seeks reality, all that is impermanent must pass away from his consciousness, so that he holds only to the Eternal Verities of which these phantasies are but flickering shadows sent to teach him to search for the real.

At the heart of every delight lies the germ of reality which leads man to seek the perpetuation of this delight. It is but a toy given to a child to teach him to yearn for the reality it represents, as a girl is given a doll to teach her to long for children and to love their care. So life offers us the symbols of Eternal Things but breaks them in our hands lest we believe them real. Neither love, nor joy, nor happiness, nor work can remain eternally to comfort us in this realm of the unreal lest we give our heart to the world of shadows and fail to seek the world of reality where lies our heritage.

Love unspeakable, joy unbelievable, peace unbreakable await us in the realms of God. But we must first give back all the tokens we have gathered here before we may reach upward to that which awaits us there. St. Paul said: "When a man is grown he puts away childish things." So the soul when it reaches its maturity turns away from the treasures of this world, of this life, to the treasures of Eternity.

These things should be understood. First that the mark of spiritual power is not phenomena, not clairvoyance, not the Siddhis. It is radiance—a clear white light which shines about the personality like a halo. It may be sensed by those who make the effort.

Second, it is not intellect but wisdom which marks the Teacher—wisdom coming from the heart, from the understanding of life and of human consciousness. This comes to those who *live*—more often therefore in the lowly. It may be sensed by those who wish, by the sense of tender understanding and sympathy for the humbler souls which radiate.

Third, there must be spiritual insight—not clairvoyance, which is only an extension of sight, nor clairaudience, which is an extension of hearing, but spiritual penetration which permits a soul to see to the heart of reality, to recognize true living values and to strip others of the veils of illusion and delusion which enfold the personality.

Spiritual power desires no authority. seeks no positions, asks nothing—seeks but to light the flame within another heart, the flame of spiritual fire which burns away the personal self.

These are the marks of spiritual potency, not those that feed the desires of the personality, not those that exalt the mind, not those that manifest phenomena.

The day has come when many shall rise to speak in the name of the Rulers of the Planet. It is essential that one should learn to discern the true from the false. Nay, more. The Masters Themselves are walking today among men— unrecognized. unvalued. because many times They come in simple garb, and in simple form for a special work. What is the mark of masters and disciples and initiates? That they recognize only one authority—the Higher Self—"unto thine own self be true". That they serve without hope of reward, recognition or position; that they are not diverted by criticism or personal pride and most that they carry the fire of spiritual things with them—joy, assurance, peace, compassion. power, insight.

A word on compassion.   The Christ is no sentimentalist.
He is a living flame, a lightning flash of white light.   It is His
office to withstand all evil forces—nothing can withstand His
power.   But destructive forces are here for a purpose and they
must fulfill that purpose.   They are needed in the development of human consciousness and power.   A man must win
his divinity.   It is not bestowed upon him.

He enters human life to risk failure and damnation to
attain the crown of the creative mind.   Only as he conquers
evil in himself and in the elemental worlds can he achieve.
He must be exposed to evil, but he must conquer.

From the throes of agony shall arise power; from the darkness shall come light; from renunciation shall come peace;
and *only* through renunciation can come peace.   Many are
not yet ready for peace.   Its very stillness, its very quiet disturbs them, for they yearn for the turbulence of emotional
and astral life.   The more delicate and ethereal play of consciousness which comes in music, beauty, art, poetry, friendship cannot satisfy them.   Yet these are part of the gifts
vouchsafed by peace.

When the soul has passed through broken and troubled
waters, when pain and anguish and agony of mind and body
have done their work, man is ready to turn away from
turmoil at any price and seek peace.   Then is he ready to
enter the spiritual life, then only can he value and appreciate
it.   Earlier it would have been unsatisfying.   For heaven is
not the satisfaction of the senses.   It is, on the contrary, the
starvation of the senses and the satisfaction of the spirit.

Many young souls cannot enter Heaven consciously even
after death, for they have as yet no capacity for enjoyment
of those things which Heaven offers.   They have not un-
furled the pinions of the spirit wherewith to soar into the

realms of God. They are still Earth-bound. For these are made the Earth-born Paradises which are established in the astral worlds as playgrounds of the child souls of the race.

Not here can heavenly joys be found—not here, but in that realm where man reveals his true divinity, his radiant Augoides. For this, when man shall know himself divine and display that divinity in all its brilliant panoply of spiritual power—for this alone is all our long and anguished pilgrimage through aeon upon aeon of time. To learn slowly to unfurl the pinions of the spirit is evolution through grosser matter undertaken. This end alone is worthy of achievement. This end alone brings peace. This is the goal of all humanity, the fulfillment of God's plan for man.

Know the Law. Obey it as must the servants of the Law who have pledged service to it. Greater than God, profounder than the abyss of Hell, mightier than the Suns in their courses is the Law—and before it does all creation bow.

Obey the Law. That only is demanded of the Lords of Light and those who seek to serve Their will. Inexorable, irrevocable, just, supreme, unchanging, and existing in all time and space—aye and in that darkness where there is no time or space—this is the Law, the Word of the Unknown Power which rules all. Only by Its Laws may it be known. Study the Laws which are eternal and through them shall come the faint glimmer of Eternal Truth.

In all generations, in all Powers, in all Planets, in all Universes, to the Great Law, all show undying reverence.

It is That for which the Masters seek. It is That which the Solar Deities seek to realize. It is That for which the whole scheme of the Universes is come into being to teach.

To the Law are all things known. By the Law are all

things possible. Bend before It in profoundest reverence and submission when you glimpse Its presence, for greater than the greatest God, more terrible than the profoundest gloom, more beautiful than love, more radiant than light, more exquisite than dawn, more ethereal than perfume, more pure than the heart of a child—The Law transcends all things.

Seek for It and if you find It, bow before Its Majesty wheresoever and howsoever It be expressed. As we learn to fulfill the Law, so do we learn to know ourselves, our universe, our work, and God. So only do we achieve power, love, and faith, for the Law is good.

Obey—Servants of the Law—Obey!

CPSIA information can be obtained
at www.ICGtesting.com
Printed in the USA
LVHW081521110123
736455LV00016B/980